Religion, Ethnicity, and Self-Identity

Salzburg Seminar books address global, contemporary issues in the arts, education, business, law, government, and science.

Religion, Ethnicity, and Self-Identity

Nations in Turmoil

Martin E. Marty and R. Scott Appleby,
Editors

1997

SALZBURG SEMINAR
Published by University Press of New England
Hanover and London

SALZBURG SEMINAR
Published by University Press of New England,
Hanover, NH 03755
© 1997 by Salzburg Seminar
Printed in the United States of America

5   4   3   2   1

CIP data appear at the end of the book

Contents

Contributors

Martin Marty (Chair)	Fairfax M. Cone Distinguished Service Professor of the History of Modern Christianity, University of Chicago
Ziad Abu-Amr	Associate Professor of Political Science, Birzeit University, West Bank
Nathan Glazer	Professor of Education and Social Structure (emeritus), Harvard University, Massachusetts
Raymond Grew	Professor of History, University of Michigan
T. N. Madan	Professor of Sociology (emeritus), Institute of Economic Growth, University of Delhi
Martha Brill Olcott	Professor of Political Science, Colgate University, New York
Gabriel Partos	Eastern Europe Analyst, BBC World Service, London

Religion, Ethnicity, and Self-Identity

Introduction: The Role of Religion in Cultural Foundations of Ethnonationalism

Martin E. Marty

A Global Context for a Global Issue

After World War II and toward midcentury, global strategists, war-makers, and peace seekers seemed to agree that the basic unit for creating conflict on the world scene was the nation. At the same time, the invention of the United Nations and its correlate organizations was an address to the problem of nationalism through the instrument of international-ism. The nations did not live or act independently of each other. The cold war, then starting, found them clustered, by force or necessity, around the agencies of the Soviet Union versus the United States. The destinies of uncommitted nations in a third world were also connected with those of the superpowers. Entities smaller than nations—call them peoples, tribes, groups, subcommunities, or whatever—existed as before but were not central in reckonings of power.

At the end of the century the nations and the United Nations survive, but their power has been compromised or undercut by forces that had been latent or suppressed; however, in the course of the decades they have resumed their old stances of opposition to each other and, often, military conflict. In the course of time the term *ethnonationalism* emerged to relate to this reality. Ethnonationalism offers much to the people who make up the "peoples," just as the peoples in their various groupings serve as a threat to peace in dozens of regions and situations.

Meanwhile, at and after midcentury, those who made what we might call mainstream assessments of the spiritual situation, the humanistic aspects of "the human condition," tended to converge with their descriptions of nations, tribes, and individuals as "secular." This did not mean that no Buddhists or Hindus, no Sikhs or Muslims, no Christians or Jews were left in the world. According to some estimates halfway through the period, in 1970 there were 1.25 billion nominal Christians, 564 million Muslims, 477 million Hindus, 237 million Buddhists, and 14 million Jews. One rattles off these figures aware that the mere mention of numbers can glaze the eye and dull the mind. Yet the intent is the opposite: to suggest that a vast number of humans arranged their lives by some sort of transcendent set of symbols and often through organization of religious groups devoted to them.

Few, however, regarded these huge religious clusters or the people who made them up to be especially promising or volatile elements in national, subnational, or international politics and military affairs. They had to do with otherworldliness and the life to come, escape into heaven or nirvana, coming to terms with personal problems and forming of local communities. But where "separation of church and state" had not disempowered them, new secular-minded, often military governments edged them toward public insignificance. Observers in European and American academic centers, often reflecting the secularity of the ambiance and ethos around them or of their personal outlooks, tended to dismiss religion in public life. However one defined the secular, it somehow included the notion that in the life of nations, especially when it came to territorial, economic, political, and social life, one could be indifferent to God or the gods, to the claim of the religious that they were dealing with ultimate reality and that it somehow impinged on affairs here and now.

That rather serene secular ethos came to be challenged in recent decades by resurgences of old religions and the births of new ones. However they thought or acted in what we might call the practical and operational sides of their lives, billions of people in the passional sides responded to ancient scriptures and modern prophetic calls. Quiescent faiths found new opportunities to refashion themselves under charismatic leadership. As old ideologies such as Soviet communism imploded, people in the West often called into question the rationalism of the eighteenth-century Enlightenment, with whose worldview they had been living. Citizens of the poor world, progressively free of colonialism, were also free to seek new patterns of meaning, often in religious renewals. There were inevitable repercussions in the fields of geopolitics.

Religion, most of the time for most people, is not an instrument for killing. People are religious, they say and their faiths promise, as part of their effort to find peace, *shalom*, communion, consolation, and integration into systems of meaning and belonging. When they thus pursue the connections of their faiths, they tend to restrict their expressions to private life. Sociologists of religion, world historians, and theologians during the decades of renewal at first saw them primarily in this light.

A second look, however, revealed that the same elements that made religion a consoler and healer could be turned into weaponry of disruption and killing. It was religion in this form that came to prevail in the combination that this book calls religious ethnonationalism. Departments of state and international agencies, long able to overlook private religion, were unable to neglect the explosion of public faith and aggressive action. Books on international affairs that at midcentury mentioned religion only slightly, if at all, were replaced by those that began to pay attention to it, as television and newspaper reporters also had to do.

What we have lacked is analytic material in the form of scholarly exposition of some of the underlying impulses of religious ethnonationalism. This book joins a modest but growing company of studies of the subject; its authors and editors hope to make a distinctive contribution to the colloquia that deal with it.

Self-Identity and Peoplehood as an Issue

A book must stand on its own and make sense on its own. Yet now and then the plot of a book can be illuminated by reference to the events that occasioned it. This book exists because of two seminars held at Salzburg, Austria, in the successive summers of 1993 and 1994. Almost nothing is as boring, alienating, or forbidding as detailed reference to a seminar at which most readers will not have been participants. Since the essays in this book, to this not unprejudiced editorial eye, are not boring, alienating, or forbidding, I shall deal with the seminars in several paragraphs and get them out of the way. There is a central point to make; I think it will be a clarifying one. It can serve as a kind of code-cracker for the themes of this book.

In 1993 the seminar was called "Ethnicity, Cultures and the Making of Nations." Scholars and doers and scholar-doers from many of the world's areas of conflict gathered at the American Studies Seminar at Schlosz Leopoldskron in Salzburg. There they addressed the ways in which "peoplehood," in the forms of the ethnic and racial groups mentioned above, for better and for worse complicated the experiences of cultures that, taken together, coexist as nations.

The seminar participants that year dealt with the conflicts that preceded and outlasted the period in which nations were dominant expressions. These tended to be conflicts that rose because peoples—we might, with some hesitancy, call them tribes—within a nation or across national boundaries could not get along with each other or had designs on each other. One could call the event of 1993 a seminar with a secular accent, *secular* being defined as above; in such a case *secular* meant that the religious dimensions of culture and the cultural dimensions of religion were not prime on the agenda. In fact, but one part of one day in two weeks was given to the religious theme.

On that part of that day, I was asked to address the religion-and-ethnicity theme. I am making no claims for the charism of the speaker or the quality of the lecture, but it is important to report that many seminar participants reacted positively to the topic. Some of them expressed relief that at last the subtopic of religion had been given due prominence, since it colored all the other themes "where they came from" and when they came together. Others found the address to the religious theme to be an almost startling innovation, so accustomed were they to slighting it when discussing ethnonationalism. In any case, they and the planners for the next year's seminar concurred on a point. They agreed that this was, indeed, an overlooked theme and merited more than a day's notice. Come back next year, came an instant invitation, and prompt participants in a second seminar to make religion a main theme.

So it was that in 1994 religion did indeed receive fair treatment, this time alongside "ethnicity" and "self-identity." While this book is not a publishing of the mere proceedings of that seminar—some of the authors were not even present—it does reflect concerns manifested there; and it benefits from such reflection, with a good deal of reworking in the light of the passage of two or three years.

The point of the conference reference, then, was to suggest that in much talk about nationalism, ethnicity, tribalism, and peoplehood in the twentieth century, there had been a great lack that needed address. Religion was not accorded the notice it must receive if diplomats, military people, mass communicators, and the general public are to make sense of one of the most volatile expressions around the globe as the century ends.

Now, religion can be connected with almost anything on the scene, for examples, the blessing of cannon, the development of institutions, the education of the young in the ways of war and peace, the nurturing of philosophies of tolerance and intolerance, or the costumery of tribes. But in the present case religion, in broad definition, is accorded notice because it connects with the concept of "self-identity" as a factor in human struggles to make sense of group life. This is especially the case in instances having to do with what is signaled in this book's subtitle: "Nations in Turmoil."

As for self-identity, the interest here is not in personal development of the sort spoken of by psychologists when they deal with, for instance, an "identity crisis." Instead, the focus is on related issues: How do groups find and express their identity? What holds them together? What motivates their actions, including their internal and external conflicts? What happens when such an identity is blurred or its holders are made insecure by what is here designated as "transition," change occurring within the social forms they had known?

Many historians have noted how intense the issue of group or social identity has become after industrialization, urbanization, migration, or mass communication—to take but four *-ation* words to describe modern processes—came or come along to disrupt presumably static or slow-to-change rural or village cultures. Other scholars have focused on what happens when national boundaries that had been imposed by colonial powers did not match the boundaries as these had been traditionally and informally drawn by the groupings they called tribes. Still other students of the scene have dealt with self-identity in crises that looked to those who faced them as being rich with opportunities. Instances of these occurred, for example, when the colonial powers went home and when new nations had occasion to develop and did emerge.

The social groupings in which the issue of self-identity is of interest in respect to nations in turmoil are much larger than is the intimate family. These may be explicitly religious, in instances where sacral, ritual, and institutional expressions are all prominent. Thus, to all appearances, self-identity is rendered secure in, say, Shi'ite Islam or Pentecostalism or Orthodoxy, in whatever nation one finds it. You do not have to ask members of such societies about their identity since so much is prescribed for them and boundaries are securely set.

Second, the social form may be tribal, though *tribe* is a word whose usage calls forth some apology. The concept of the tribe was invented far from the people to whom the word was applied. Normally, it was brought by anthropologists or other outsiders to peoples who did not call themselves tribes. But the tribe can be seen, as Eugen Rosenstock-Huessy saw it, to be the *couche*, the matrix of values. Such a tribe is the unit larger than the family, the locale where transmission of the culture goes on, in many ways independently of national boundaries.

Third, self-identity occurs in the polis, the human city that is larger than the tribe, where pluralism begins to manifest itself. There is tremendous variety in ancient Sparta or modern Singapore, yet there were people identifiable as Spartans and there are Singaporeans, people who have something more than mere shared space that they hold in common. And beyond religious, tribal, and political boundaries, there are the nations themselves, invented as we know them in modern forms, which means in modern times.

The same person may gain self-identity or find it threatened in any one of these four kinds of units or in combinations of any two or more of them. But however they get interrupted by the intrusive scholar, we do observe them being busy, implicitly and sometimes explicitly asking: "Who am I? What do or should I do? To whom do I belong? How shall I act? What habits are appropriate? Whom shall I trust? How do I describe myself? How am I empowered?" These are enduring, classical themes. While through the ages most people did not use the self-identity term, they have wrestled with it in some form or other always and everywhere, according to the testimony of paleontologists, archaeologists, classicists, historians, and social psychologists.

One can observe the struggling, the wrestling, about self-identity from several vantages. The closer one gets to the people, the more vivid and tangible is the religious component. Often I like to compare levels of social scientific observation to hurricane watching. From a great distance, as from a satellite, human movements may represent great and elegant swirls of motion. These are undifferentiated, viewed from that distance. It is impossible to observe or detail from such a height. Thus, in the present case scholars have observed trends like modernization, secularization, or nationalization as global phenomena and treated them with a high level of generalization. When that is the case, religion will not stand out unless the observer makes a point of reminding herself and others that it is an elusive yet powerful presence.

Second, the identity of the hurricane is different from the aspect of the C-130 aircraft from which meteorologists do their watching in the very eye of the storm. Here the force of wind and cloud and rain is much more apparent, and detail begins to appear. Compare this vantage to that of the sociologists who study large cultures up close. One thinks of the decisive pioneer sociologists of religion like Max Weber, Emile Durkheim, and Georg Simmel. In their writings, religious themes such as "the Protestant ethic" or religious "collective representation" begin to stand out, but the level of generalization is still very broad and high.

The third point of vantage for observing the storms of change is the ground level. Now one pays attention to the people who are up close, people who possess information and perspective but must stay on the scene. In the hurricane world, this company includes bridge tenders, medical personnel, fire and police forces, and radio and television broadcasters. They are close enough to the storm to know what is happening. They thus have some advantages over those who do not have access to the instruments they employ. In our analogy, at this level one would spy religious professionals, the shamans and gurus, the priests and scribes and scholars. They know the place of religion, but can they place it in larger contexts? They are familiar with the experience of the people in the huts, who are positioned where the hurricane will hit.

Religion, fourth, is most vivid to and visible in the figurative huts. There in the face of storms, such as those occasioned by "modernity" or by something similar that appears under other labels, people find themselves confronting very few choices. They can flee or they can "batten down the hatches" and gather the sandbags as they nail plywood over the windows. Translated to our field of inquiry, one can say that their search for self-identity, when it is challenged by change, may very well include recourse to religion, perhaps even as a starting and end point. In fact, religion may be the prime motivator, inspirer, and legitimator of their seeking and their acting.

Today, despite or perhaps as a part of a global communications revolution, there is more access to and curiosity about the mentality of the people in the huts than there had been back when it was easy to screen out their concerns while talking about distantly observed global trends. Who could have foreseen these trends in the face of the great events and inventions of the times? This is the century of assault on personal and smaller-group identity, thanks to totalitarianisms, coerced mass movements, bureaucratization, and the attempt by hegemonous powers in government and business to manufacture uniformity and obedience.

This is also the century in which many of the promises of modernization and secularization were to have been fulfilled—to satisfy the minds of people and to enrich their experience. Most of the observers and anticipators who were shaped by the Western Enlightenment—and they do not live only in the West—did not foresee the trends. I mentioned uncertainty about the Enlightenment a few paragraphs ago; it is now the place to see what that wavering has to do with observations about religion. In the eyes and reflexes of most of them—most of us?—it was assumed that in the course of modern history, whenever observers would monitor the various human cultures, they would find less religion than they had recognized in the same settings a year or a decade earlier. As anyone who consults the prophecies and reports will confirm, it also was assumed that whatever of religion survived would be mild, concessive, ecumenical, tolerant, and capable of breeding little more than indifference. It would certainly be too powerless to help contribute to people in their struggles to find and express self-identity. Such religion would certainly be too bland and negotiable for people to use when they were in conflict, too weak to be able to inspire aggressive action.

Most books of prophecy missed the point that has become clear now, near the end of the century, the end of the millennium. It turns out that most of the antireligious totalitarianisms are long gone. China, North Korea, and Cuba, in their own very different ways, are among the few exceptions. The bipolar concept of nations massed on both sides of an iron curtain or a set of walls is not available for a creative address to the world situation today. Instead, small nations and the tribes within them or the social groups that transgress the imposed boundaries of nations are the main agents of wars. Those who study such human groupings are more likely than before to try to do justice to the religions within each. Their studies have in fact grown urgent: if things "go wrong" on the self-identity front, anomie results or conflict within nations occurs. We are sometimes told that 100 percent of the current wars can be called "civil," and religion in them has to be interpreted in civil war terms.

On the other hand, if things "go right" on the self-identity front, human conditions can improve and more people can realize some measures of peace and justice. In such cases a religious dimension is likely to be apparent. The faith communities generally are responsive to texts that talk about shalom, peace, reconciliation, and they have some potential for countering the impulses in religions to induce conflict.

When Religion-and-Ethnicity Get Ignored

In the act of contrasting periods and emphases, there is no point in trying to establish that the present scene is unique, that never before have people used religion to legitimate their search for self-identity or their action as peoples. Such use of religion may be an integral part of the human condition and closely associated with definitions of religion. It is remarkable and remark-worthy here for two reasons.

First, as already suggested, many thoughtful people assumed that religious faith and practice would disappear, if indeed they had not already permanently disappeared from sectors of the modern scene. On the assumption that it is better to be educated and informed about a scene than not, they tend to welcome whatever helps them alter the old assumptions.

Second, when new religions appear or old ones get revitalized, they lack the roots of traditional faiths. This means that the people who profess them are more innovative, frenetic, unstable, and capable of erratic actions than are adherents of half-compromised "old-time religions." During the six and more years that co-editor R. Scott Appleby and I directed the Fundamentalism Project for the American Academy of Arts and Sciences, we often found scholars who asked why we did not study fundamentalist-like movements of centuries ago. The formula that worked best was this: we were studying only those that took shape *after* people in the Western academy said there could be no more of such. So it is with religious ethnonationalism. Everyone who is at all familiar with the record of people once called "primitive" knew that religion informed tribal life. One could make a profitable historical study of that background. But we are looking at tribes that drew upon or exploited faith and practices relating them to the sacred *after* the intellectuals of the West thought that the day for such had passed.

This is not the place to engage in a full-scale description of the forces that led to religion's being obscured nor to define modernity and modernization. Whoever listens to the rhetoric of the ayatollahs, rabbis, priests, and pastors who call attention to religion and who often exploit it, "modernity" is a kind of code word for any of the erosive forces that threaten self-identity.

Some who observe the scene might conclude that technological change is vital to the disruption of faith communities. But almost at once it becomes clear that many intense and tribal religionists have adapted well to it. Instead, they are more threatened by other concomitants of modernization trends. These would certainly include elements of differentiations and specializations of sorts that had often sequestered religion and kept it distant from public affairs. What we might think of as an unsigned, subtle, informal modern pact dictated the terms. In effect, it allowed religion to remain on the scene as long as its adherents were content to be restricted to the private and leisure sphere. In that refuge it was differentiated from cultural, social, political, and economic sorts of activity.

Second, pluralism of sorts accompanied political freedom, human migration, and an awareness of the "other" as it was stimulated and informed by mass media. To illustrate: it had been one thing for the Christian to missionize and seek to convert the bad Buddhist far away; but it was another, a more confusing one, when this "other," this different one, moved next door to the Christian and proved to be the good Buddhist, someone who enjoyed her own rights of self-expression and expressed herself well. How, one asks, could a common identity be sustained among those who must share space and a rostrum with her?

For a third parallel aggravation, relativism was often a corollary of pluralism. In its instance, everything and everyone claimed to be equally true and trustworthy, which could also mean that they were also equally false and unreliable. Therefore, many people retreated from the danger zones where they might be exposed to the other. They formed self-defensive and then aggressive enclosed groups.

Why in such kinds of activities and bondings were the religious dimensions consequently so often overlooked? There have to be many reasons. We have already implied that formal philosophies or reflexive habits associated with modernization or secularization were partly responsible. Many of the specialist observers had in their autobiographies a personal experience of having moved from defined adolescent religious participation to critical and skeptical adulthood. Then it was tempting, even natural, for them to dismiss religion as belonging to an earlier stage of their own development and of the human race in general. Or they found it efficient to try to restrict religion to the private and thus irrelevant sphere. Some of them worked against backgrounds of an implicit metaphysics of progress and with it a loss of religion. Urgent agendas of economic and commercial sorts preoccupied still others.

Let it be noted ironically that one finds this loss of attention to the religious factor in ethnicity and self-identity more apparent precisely among the elites whose business it is to provide realistic pictures of human action. These include scholars, reporters, commercial leaders, and often politicians. That situation is changing; as a colleague has put it, "the departments of state have 'got religion'" or are beginning to "get religion." This does not mean that the people who make up these elites are necessarily turning more religious than before, though that may sometimes be the case. What is more important to note is that many have grown in their awareness of the religious factor in war and peace.

Occasions for Recent Awakenings to the Issue

The reader of this book will quickly see how, across the globe, circumstances have risen that lead people to pay more attention to the religious connection than before. Consulting any day's newspaper or taking advantage of access to electronic media will serve immediately as alerts. Here is a bold example: today adjectives like *communist* or *nationalist* are less likely to be associated with an army, a terrorist group, or a peacemaking team than are words like "Jewish militant," "Muslim fundamentalist," or "Christian Coalition."

The Styles of Religions That Are Assertive Today

We have spoken in ways that could give the impression that religion is all one thing, everywhere alike. On the contrary, religion, however defined, takes many forms in diverse cultures. It may be, and often in Western industrialized forms has become, an element that many regard as reminiscent of earlier civilizations. It looks monumental and ossified, culturally passive, inert except for some almost meaningless ceremonial purposes. But religious faith and practice may also be and in much of the world have become innovative, prospective, culturally active, and patently usable for political purposes, many of them instrumental in the search for self-identity. Religious styles may be the result of acts of retrieval from the past, developed into new creations, such as fundamentalisms tend to be.

They may also be NRMs (new religious movements), forms that are sometimes, against the will of their leader and to their displeasure, called cults. They may seem to be free-standing or they quickly can become attached to or can inspire political and military causes and live by connection and coalition with them. The latter expression most bears watching.

Similarly, another set of two forms of religion present themselves. One is conventional religion of the sort regarded as "mainstream" in the various "world religions." This is the kind of religion one encounters in encyclopedias of religion, textbooks, yearbooks, guidebooks, atlases, and gazetteers. In American culture we might think of it as "Religion on the Yellow Pages" of the phone book. On those pages diverse beckonings of competitively advertising religious congregations and denominations vie for attention.

Alongside these, however, there are also unconventional religions of many sorts, most of them named by social scientists and not always called religious by their adherents. Among these can be the forms of "civil religion" discerned by Durkheim, Jean-Jacques Rousseau, and their modern disciples. They can be called public religion of a sort sought and advocated by founders like those of the United States, including Benjamin Franklin, who coined the term. They may be the creation and bond of the Orthodox parties in Israel or the Shi'ite ayatollahs in Iran and elsewhere. This unconventional religion, the kind not housed in familiar institutions, may assume folk and popular forms, replete with rites that parallel the now-neglected or forbidden ceremonies of religions that had long been identified with particular cultures. Such religion attaches itself to sports, work, entertainment, gambling ventures—and tribal claims for defined self-identities.

It would be futile to seek and to offer an agreed upon definition of religion in all four of these cases. But it is possible to acquire the phenomenologists' habits and begin by observing and pointing. What, one then begins by asking, are the phenomena that have long been called religious and that manifest themselves today under several guises and in many modes? Almost arbitrarily I would point to factors like those among peoples seeking and expressing ethnonationalism or searching for self-identity through tribal religiosity:

Whatever else it involves, what we observe as religion is a testimony to the experience of the sacred, a response to hierophany or revelation in word, vision, or mystical expression. If movements lack claims on otherness, the awe-inspiring, the sacred, as they make drastic claims on human loyalty, they quickly come to appear soulless, or they ossify or fade. Thus, Saddam Hussein was not able to turn the Gulf War into a credible jihad in the eyes of most other leaders in the Muslim world. His call for participation in a war that he wanted to call holy rang hollow in the ears of others who saw in him no such evidences of awe before the sacred.

Second, religions tend to take social and eventually institutionalized form. In industrialized nations there tend now to be some strong trends toward "privatization," but in most of the world religion is a communal expression. People with whom we associate the word *religious* display compulsions to testify, proselytize, act together, share experience, and perform aggressively. For all that, not privatized but social forms of religion, common faiths, alone will serve.

In the eyes of the philosopher, next, religion will appear to express "ultimate concern" and thus will represent what those who profess it will regard as nonnegotiable. That is why religion is such a baffling and benumbing puzzle to those who, attuned to the ways of conventional statecraft, seek to promote some compromise, some yielding among parties in conflict. Religion serves to help people and peoples create for themselves a world more real than the ordinary one. They will engage in suicide missions because they are assured of the reality of their immediate transit to paradise upon their death.

Further indicators include the fact that religious people and peoples tend to favor mythic and symbolic expression over straightforwardly rationalistic and pragmatic forms. They also engage in ritual and ceremonial practices as they go through the seasons, the passages of life, the sequence of crises to which they must respond. One will ordinarily hear from them formal or informal philosophical rationales for the religious commitments. We can call these metaphysical suggestions, urging that behind the curtain of the manifest world there is a bigger one that can be used for explanation. And, of course, behavioral correlates will follow: religious leaders will urge adherents to make peace or take up the sword. Believers should observe this ceremony or refrain from eating that food.

To all of these elements add the instinct for setting boundaries: "we" are in and "you" are out. Here are the faithful and there the infidels. God is behind this group but remote from moderates and people who cross boundaries. Such are the claims.

The Surprising Character of These Manifestations Today

If it is true that the phenomenologist points more than she defines when encountering religious or quasi-religious phenomena, she also need do little more than point to show how diverse are the expressions. First to be observed is the growth of world religions. Most of them are weathered by exposure to each other or by the buffeting winds of modernities, however these are defined. But within each of them, be they Hindu or Muslim, Buddhist or Christian, Jewish or Sikh, are revitalization movements whose participants are not content to endure this weathered existence. They turn aggressive and innovative and become the forms that are growing most rapidly, most surprisingly.

Most of the new religions include in their mission the supplementing or supplanting of the traditional faiths. These evidently offer more satisfaction to people seeking identity than do the well-worn ones that refuse to demonize the enemies of or the mere alternatives to their claims.

In a third case, leaders can refashion old religions for present purposes. Thus, after seven decades of Soviet discouragement and suppression of religion, Christian Orthodoxy has been offered a new chance. The new Orthodoxy often makes its way by evoking ancient Russophilic (and too often, anti-Semitic) tendencies. These had been suppressed or at least hidden from view, neglected, and forgotten in the years between 1917 and 1989. After the end of the Soviet Union, Christian fundamentalists who had earlier been forced to retreat from the public sphere came back with a vengeance in the last third of the century. They often based their claims on their ability to provide a self-identity. They were able to gain power over parts of their nation and, in some cases, eventually to "run" it, in terms theologically satisfying to them.

Whether in conventional religions that had been turned to support of peoplehood and nationalisms in transit or in unconventional and new faiths, religion characteristically fortifies and inspires the new tribal and national movements. Once more, it is hard to discern many envisionings of this kind of an end-of-the-century dominant trend in the writings of social scientists, theologians, or prophets, even after midcentury. The belligerents come to the scene as surprises—if not to the locals in their huts, then to cosmopolitans who view them from satellite or airplane distances.

A word must be said about the possibilities of misperceiving and mislabeling movements and their characteristics. One may well find reasons to be economical and cautious in acts of naming, to resist impulses to denominate all kinds of things religious, or quasi- or para- or pseudoreligious. One might say: if everything is religious, then nothing is religious. In the case of ethnonationalism, for instance, it is important to do justice to nonreligious elements. Tribal hatreds, economic interests, territorial disputes, historical slights remembered, obscure occasions for malice—all these can motivate the wars in the former Yugoslavia or Rwanda or elsewhere. Or religion can be epiphenomenal, one more factor thrown in for purposes of analysis after all the decisive (e.g., economic and territorial) components have been included. But even if scholars proceed with caution and keep these reservations and qualifiers in mind, they will not lack subject matter to be denominated religious and essential to the story of peoplehood.

Similarly, there are reasons to resist reductionisms. With that term we refer to moves that most would call religious, but to the reductionist they are "nothing but" expressions of class, market interests, natural human aggression, psychological traumas, projections, and the like. It is difficult if not impossible to disprove or qualify the results of all efforts at reduction. Obviously, religion has a great deal to do with psychological impulses and ethnic or national groupings. Indeed, if it did not, we would not be discussing it here and not fashioning this book-length argument, with its many evidences. But it is valid to bracket this form of the "hermeneutics of suspicion," this mode of interpretation that is wary of letting religion stand as an independent category. At some stage, to be fair to a phenomenon, one must suspend the reductionist impulse enough so that the religious dimensions are at least from the start taken seriously on their own terms. One need not be committed to the notion that each person is *homo religiosus*, integrally and inevitably religious, to take seriously the claims of those who think they are being religious or whose words and actions match those associated with religion.

The Most Intense Forms of Religion Are Most Useful for Self-Identity

Earlier we mentioned that both the quantity and the quality of late-twentieth-century religion in ethnonationalism and the quest for self-identity have surprised many observers. About its quantity there can be little argument: the headlines make that clear. As to the quality, we noted that it was intense religious expression that prospered in an age that was supposed to have been rational, cosmopolitan, religiously serene. In open competition, innovative fundamentalisms or inventive traditionalisms outpace their concessive competitors within world religions everywhere.

Here one might profitably introduce the term *fanaticism*, as long as it is remembered that there can be fanatic humanisms and secularisms just as, obviously, there have been fanatic impositions of antireligious ideologies in many regimes. Fanatically held-to religions have a great appeal today at the expense of those that inspire tolerance, that lead people to say to others, "You may have a point" or "Let's engage in dialogue." We recall the roots of the word *fanatic*. The *fanum* is the shrine, the temple, the sacred space. The *pro + fane* person is someone who steps outside or exists outside that space. The fanatic is someone who is habitually too close to the fanum and loses perspective. It has been said that fanaticisms tend to be variations on the same phenomenon—in the case of this book, on self-identity and ethnicity. Only their object varies. Thus, fanatic Shi'ite, Jewish, Sikh, and Christian movements often called fundamentalism are *really* different from each other, at least in respect to their substance. But it is chiefly the substance that provides the variations. The forms, the ways in which each is approached and upheld, on the other hand, are what provide the distinctives. The object, in this case one's own people, tribe, or nation, attracts the fanatic's ability to develop jealous, vengeful, and focused faith in respect to its sacred aspect.

Fanaticisms prosper in times of cultural upheaval, of calls for revolution and sacrifice, jihad and crusade and holy war. In the eyes of pluralists and cosmopolitans, who bring their own weaknesses to the scene, the world of the many nations, tribes, and peoples, if they are interactive, can be perceived as enriching. Fanatic religion reinforces tendencies to the exclusive. In that temper, people assert that only "our" gods and "our" people are privileged and sacred. You, the other, are "pro + fane" and should exist "outside" the territory, if at all. "Ethnic cleansing," then, usually acquires or is moved by religious justifications.

The Essays in This Book

Before turning to the elaborations of these themes and to the case studies that follow, it is in place to remind readers that here we are not talking about the ways in which religion can promote dialogue, can motivate conversation. This is a book with a one-sided emphasis. Totally neglected here are the healing, consoling, saving, and integrating sides of religion, which, as mentioned above, are what normally draw people to one or another of the faiths. Most adherents do not "join" Islam to achieve a political end. They already share a Muslim worldview, and then circumstances or beckoning leaders offer rewards for participation in some movement or other that may come across to adherents as being salvific or therapeutic. But they then get called out to engage in holy acts against the "other."

Second, there is no assumption that the current scene is the full and final unfolding of human history. Intense and hard-line religions will not necessarily remain so; most of the world religions, full of compromise as they have become, began fanatically and usually in identification with a single people before they went international and ecumenical. There are some reasons, not a few of them economic, that lead many in the peoples and nations to adapt, compromise, assimilate, and become virtuosos at survival.

Also undernoted here is the fact that while elites are often drawn to leadership of ethnonationalist movements and know how to exploit and distort the struggle for self-identity, many who join are from the beleaguered "huts." Peacemakers and adjudicators will get nowhere unless they realize the aggrieved state of many who are drawn to prefer the hard-line religions that provide the self-identity that cosmopolitans take for granted or live without having clarified.

Raymond Grew first deals with a religious species of the ethnonationalist genus or, as scholars with another specialty might prefer to say, an ethnonationalist species of a religious, specifically fundamentalist, genus. He goes into more detail than does this introduction on the question why and why now, in respect to hard-line religious movements. His version of the importance of religion at the opening of his essay is a key not only to it but to much that follows in subsequent chapters. He so successfully situates the impulse toward fundamentalism in the scope of people today that momentarily one may wonder why anyone would choose *not* to turn fundamentalist. Especially where people are overrun by forces beyond their control and left with nothing but ambiguous, paradoxical, and self-contradictory perceptions and counsels, they seek an emphatic and clarified alternative. To his credit, then, he also goes on to see how precarious are the formulas and patterns of fundamentalisms themselves, concentrating on the necessary "balancing act" that leaders and followers alike must endure and perfect. Of special importance in the unfolding of the plots in this book is Grew's emphasis on local variations and situations. He also enters into the record a few cautionary notes about the study of fundamentalism and even about the term itself. It is not the predominant term in the subsequent chapters, but it overshadows many others or forms a subplot in them.

The choice of six "local situation" studies is by no means arbitrary. If one shades the areas on a world map where these situations prevail, it can be seen that geographical representativeness is but one of their features. Second, they are "hot spots" on which the eyes of many are focused. Third, we sought varieties of response, from "killing field" to arenas of semicivil argument. A second set of six local examples would demonstrate the intrinsic value of each and would add detail. But much of the basic global plot is revealed in these instances.

First, Ziad Abu-Amr takes up Arab Islamic fundamentalism, a movement so strong that by itself it could have placed this subject on the international agenda. Because it is strong and obvious, such Islam is subject to false universalization. That is, there is a danger of its being made into a bogey and portrayed as stronger than it is. Abu-Amr's exploration is marked by thoroughness and fairness alike and needs no qualification or elaboration here.

Second, T. N. Madan exposes to view the situation in India, where religions and nationalisms have long been fused and where intense forms of both make news these decades. His is therefore a more historical treatment than the others. It serves intrinsically for those who would make sense of India and then, beyond that, to illustrate how long trends lie behind current expressions. Islam, Hinduism, Sikhism, and to a small extent, Christianity, are on his scene and will remain on our screen for years to come.

Martha Brill Olcott, third, has a somewhat different assignment, because she has to deal with a part of the world where the religious dimension was long suppressed and about which many observers from a distance had no more than a dim awareness. She writes of what have come to be called Soviet successor states. Olcott identifies herself as someone long accused of "bourgeois falsification" because she "saw ethnicity and religion as normal elements of self-identity" and then connected this with political dimensions. The accusers are long gone, and Professor Olcott is here to survey the terrain they left behind. She includes Christian Orthodoxy and Islam as case studies.

Gabriel Partos, in a fourth case study, looks in on a world where ethnic expressions have turned into military devastations: the Balkans. For several years now and with the prospect that the case will continue into the immediate future, warfare between the peoples who once made up the artificial national entity called Yugoslavia makes news daily. Partos asks, among other things, how much a role religion plays in self-identity and nationalism, since not all the warfare is religious there. Protestantism and Judaism are small religious communities to which he pays attention, but Orthodoxy, Roman Catholicism, and Islam are the contenders in his region. "The role of religion and the religious communities cannot be ignored." There are, he says, no laboratory conditions that make possible its separation from nationalism. His extensive treatment might make a small book in itself and is certain to be regarded as valuable by any who want to make sense of the wars and tensions in the Balkans.

Finally, Nathan Glazer speaks of American multiculturalism in a case study of a nation where racism remains strong and ethnic differentiation is rich but where late in this century there have been few mass or lethal explosions of religiously legitimated ethnic contesting. While Glazer stresses the religious dimensions less than some others, it is implied, and it does color the cultural and multicultural scene. The five local case studies bring us from theory closer to the "people in the huts." Among them, religion is a more obvious factor with which to reckon.

When the New Christian Right was beginning to be observed in the United States in the 1970s, I recall being asked about how to address it from outside. The advice was dual. "Don't underestimate it"—it has staying power, motivation, and an adaptability factor that will help it prosper. Also, "Don't overestimate it"—it cannot make good on all its promises and will go through many transformations. The same advice, it seems to me, applies to those who use this book to gain a new appreciation of religion in ethnicity and the issues of self-identity. Don't underestimate such religion—people are being inconvenienced by it and killed by it, and this is likely to continue well into the next century. Don't overestimate it—there are other factors at work in a world where a global economy, computer networks, and the like serve to qualify, compromise, and often undercut religious exclusivisms and the self-identities of the people who make up a troubled world and will continue to do so.

On Seeking the Cultural Context
of Fundamentalism

Raymond Grew

If we accept that militant religious movements worldwide deserve a common name, fundamentalism is certainly the one most familiar. Two obvious questions then follow: Why have these kinds of movements prospered so widely, and why should they have done so in the latter part of the twentieth century? This chapter considers both questions and suggests that fundamentalist movements can be studied comparatively in terms of a common pattern in their development and the places in which they thrive.

The Importance of Religion

Fundamentalisms are religious movements, and modern social science tends to find their growth surprising. For centuries, theories of social change have posited that religion was in decline. Our ideas of reason and progress, the universal appeal of liberalism, the inevitability of Marxism, the inescapable disenchantment of the world, the secularization of society, and the process of modernization have all incorporated that view. A great deal of logic supports it. Personal faith in a transcendent, active God and in the mysterious efficacy of prayer and ritual would seem to become harder to sustain and less necessary as the result of historic change—change that can be measured not just in terms of ideas but by the progress of functional differentiation, rational organization, and reliance on scientific method and by the withering of ties of kinship and custom. The belief that civilization is moving in this direction, reinforced by the lamentations, rebukes, and denunciations of religious leaders, has become an assumption so widespread as to be almost invisible. Such a body of diverse, systematic, and engaged analysis is in itself historical evidence in favor of that assumption;

and the phenomenon of contemporary fundamentalism, however sweeping it is taken to be, cannot be said to refute or even undermine any of the grand schemas on which so much of current scholarship rests. Some reconsideration might suggest, however, that no one of these bodies of thought (maybe not even Marxism) really requires an evolutionary theory of religion's historic regression. (Fundamentalists, of course, proclaim that they do.) In any case, our surprise at fundamentalism's success may result more from our own assumptions than from any sudden turning in belief systems or social organization.

Note how often explanations of fundamentalism emphasize factors much like those often used to explain any number of mass movements, including nationalism, fascism, and communism. We need to ask why the movements that concern us here are religious ones and to remember that religious beliefs have always been those that people were most willing to sacrifice, fight, and die—and live—for. Apparently that remains true in the late twentieth century, at least for some people and in some places, and those places include the most modern of societies. Issues of abortion, divorce, religious education, and relations between church and state remain heated and divisive in the United States, France, Italy, and Germany, where they are battled over precisely because they engage religion. Analyses of voting behavior in all of those societies show, again and again, that religious identity is as important as or more important than class, income, occupation, or region in predicting how individuals vote.

At the very least, evidence of religion's awesome adaptability to new circumstances suggests something more than institutional tactics, theological compromise, or personal confusion. Systems of belief that connect the most intimate and personal experiences to family, to society, to a way of life, and then to universal meaning; that are logical and mystical at the same time; that are prescriptive in broad ethical terms and in minute detail can often contain and thrive on complexity and even contradiction. Constantly reinterpreted through the very act of living, the search for religious meaning makes religion adaptable. We need to explain not why religion survives but why the manifestations of it that we are calling fundamentalism should thrive around the world in the second half of the twentieth century. Exploring answers to that question can tell us a lot about our era, and the essays recently published in the volumes of the Fundamentalism Project of the American Academy of Arts and Sciences provide encouragement for doing so.[1]

The Process by Which Fundamentalism Develops and Spreads

It is helpful first to have in mind the elements that fundamentalisms seem to have in common, not so much in terms of explicit beliefs, organizations, or tactics—which vary greatly—but as movements that share in an identifiable process of growth. Then we can ask what in our era stimulates that process. Fundamentalism feeds on a community's recognition of the need to mobilize against threats to its way of life. These include but are not limited to threats to religious belief, the sacred, and the divine order. The dangers are seen as diffuse, the result of laxity as well as false ideas and of new temptations as well as formal policies; they are thought to threaten the community as well as harmony with God. Interpreted as part of a general, historical trend, these dangers come to be understood as something more than the ordinary confusions and contradictions of the human condition (for which conventional belief might seem to provide adequate guidance). The present is a moment of crisis in which all of the future is a stake in a test of personal belief and moral stamina. The outcome will reveal the power of God's will.

The individual's first protection against these historical forces and personal temptations is to accept a fundamental core of belief, doctrines, and behaviors from which there can be no deviation and no compromise, eliminating ambiguities that invite fatal laxity. Adherence to this core becomes the measure of belonging to a community (in which the painful tensions between the individual and society so characteristic of modern life are all but eliminated). These beliefs are usually said to be derived from a sacred text (as in religions of the book) but may include the introduction of new or overlooked texts, special glosses, or the statements of spiritual leaders. Such claims require an interpretive campaign to establish not only the incontrovertible meaning of these texts but also their inspiring relevance to the immediate issues of the day. In this way the great tradition of a major religion is selectively invoked and firmly attached to a specific community of believers. Like all movements of religious reformation, fundamentalisms find traditional religious institutions flabby and weak.

A fundamentalist movement then grows if it can establish and maintain its militancy while broadening its community. Evidence of commitment and power, militancy reinforces the movement's claim to be the worthy heir of its religion's great tradition, and this militancy puts the established institutions of that religion on the defensive. For fundamentalism uses the vocabulary of established religion in the name of the same ultimate purpose while proclaiming angry intransigence as proof of purity and devotion. At the same time, the recruitment of a wider membership requires building on available communal ties of kinship, ethnicity, region, nation, shared status, social practices, and common enemies. Because this process of enlarging the sense of community could lessen cohesion, growth must be accompanied by sharp markers distinguishing true believers from all others. Ritual devotions and participation in public meetings and demonstrations serve—like distinctive manners, dress, and language—this process of demarking who belongs to the expanding movement. But distinctiveness from the larger society, however useful for the community's development, is a by-product that arises from the extraordinarily specific prescriptions for daily conduct. The behavior in ordinary affairs that distinguishes fundamentalists from the rest of society is an expression of personal religious belief and of community. Its distinctiveness is taken as a sign of the community's closeness to God, but so is the movement's growth, which is accompanied by an expansion of the range of activities used to define and express community, including marriage, education, and business dealings.

Because of the tension between maintaining internal cohesion and winning broader support, fundamentalists continually tilt one way or the other, making critical choices that shape the movement, provide its leaders great tactical flexibility, and sometimes stimulate violence as the ultimate proof of devotion. The willingness to kill and readiness to die becomes definitive proof of loyalty. These patterns of growth can be studied comparatively. Fundamentalist movements can be analyzed in terms of the ways in which they relate to the dominant religion, institutionally and doctrinally; the social ties on which they build (regional, ethnic, etc.); the markers they employ (language, dress, custom); and the tactics employed and the results achieved.

Inevitably, these patterns of growth create tensions and contradictions, some of them much like those faced by earlier religious movements and some characteristic of twentieth-century fundamentalisms. Increased separation, essential to the movement's formation, is attenuated by the use of mass communication to reach a wider audience and by the selection of specific social groups as targets for recruitment because increased membership and the techniques used to win it carry their own risks. The capacity to reach a mass audience is a crucial asset that requires special skills and a participant's understanding of contemporary society if modern means of communication—pamphlets, mass meetings, radio broadcasts, and television—are to be used effectively to articulate core beliefs while addressing contemporary issues in a way that establishes a fundamentalism's relevance to the experiences and needs of a larger public. Mass communication relies on the use of striking but familiar images, verbal and graphic, while creating a useful uncertainty about how large the movement is, obscuring the line between believers and sympathizers. There is a structural problem as well. Groups organized by occupation, age, or gender risk being drawn into the established cultures of the workplace, commercial practice, school, or sport. As assimilation beckons, the resulting tension makes those distinctions of language, dress, and participation symbolically and psychologically more important, even as they may be softened. For students of fundamentalist movements, all this means that fundamentalisms can also be compared in terms of the techniques of mass communication they employ (and its effect on their own program), the specific social groups to which they reach out (and the accommodation made to them), the movement's public activities, and the causes and signs that come to be taken as the crucial sign of membership.

Who belongs, is sympathetic, or is opposed is a critical matter, tested (and redefined) almost daily. That creates pressure for ever stronger tests of loyalty, one of the factors leading to clashes with established religion, secular society, and the state. There are others. Fundamentalism promises the peace and joy of a personal and social life fully and unproblematically integrated with religious belief and practice. The emphasis on clear doctrine and firm boundaries affirms that integration as more than mere system maintenance. As the movement grows, it increasingly encounters resistance in the institutional and social practices of the larger society. Changing them comes to seem essential (although the measure of change may be increasingly delimited); pluralism and tolerance in themselves are among the threats to communal and religious life.

To survive and grow, fundamentalism must sustain an ever more complicated balance. Claiming the protection of cultural respect for religion, it must also maintain its militancy. Addressing and absorbing social and political ideas independently vital in the public arena, it must also keep its own ideas at the center of discussion. While appealing to the values of selected elites—officials, military officers, politicians, or intellectuals—it must also maintain a populist conception of community. The quality of leadership and of the decisions analysts understand as tactical are therefore critical to the movement's success. Thus, fundamentalists can be compared in terms of their tactics, the kinds of issues they raise, and the resonance they achieve in the larger society.

All of this creates a restless dynamic that is and must proclaim itself to be aggressive. Nearly any response to the movement can be made a kind of validation: indifference is impiety; resistance, abuse of power; denunciation, heresy. Violent confrontation hardens boundaries and for the movement can be a rite of initiation and a welcome test. Each society differs as to where the lines of conflict are drawn and what alliances emerge, and these patterns, too, can be fruitfully compared. The ways in which

fundamentalism finds resonance in the larger society through a process
that balances communal integration and social conflict merits comparative
analysis, which in turn may well indicate some of the essential characteristics of our age. That possibility indicates the importance of asking why
fundamentalism should be a twentieth-century phenomenon.

Fundamentalism and the Modern World

Fundamentalism's denunciation of contemporary society is one of the
ways in which these movements partake of modern life. It does not prove
that they are simply reactions against modernity, for in fact their criticisms
reflect and make use of much that is central to modern thought and modern society. Many of the ways of thinking and much of the social experience essential to fundamentalism have been so characteristic of the past
two centuries that to historians they constitute part of what distinguishes
modern history from everything that came before it. I will discuss some of
those first. Other fundamentalist concerns have become more prominent
in society in the past fifty years, and they will be treated separately.

Since the revolutions at the end of the eighteenth century that opened
a new era, modern thought has been obsessed with change. Theories of
society, conservative or radical, have been theories about the nature of
historic change, and belief that change results from large-scale historical processes has in effect become universal. The debate has been about
what those processes are, the source of their momentum, and more pointedly, how and whether they can be shaped or controlled. Fundamentalism
enters that familiar discourse on the side of human liberty. Right-thinking
people, acting collectively, can identify the sources of change and erect cultural filters that will selectively accept and reject change (the very changes
that mark modernity) as principle dictates.

Fundamentalism benefits, too, from a long tradition of semieschato-
logical movements (Christian, Marxist, positivist, and liberal) that predict
the direction of the future. In modern society many know how to establish
such a movement, and there is a public that knows its charms, but currently fundamentalism has few competitors that can match its confidence.
Even the widespread conviction that historical processes have predictable
natural tendencies can be made useful ethically. It makes a great difference,
of course, whether this process is understood as millennial or recent, is
considered consonant with or a contradiction of a given society's own history, and is seen to be propelled primarily by (in addition to God's will)
power, economics, ideas, or social benefits. Fundamentalists are remark-
ably free to mix and blend, however, for they measure change less by what

it offers than by where it will lead; and they tame change by considering its dangers part of those eternal trials that believers have always faced. Nor is this simply conservative, for the collective will when allied with God can direct history to new and higher ends. For all of this fundamentalists have a rich treasure of modern experience on which to draw, set forth in the theory and practice of scores of nineteenth- and twentieth-century movements, both utopian ones that sought to transform the world and ones that attempted to prevent or contain modernizing change. The failures and (more limited) successes of these movements can be taken to prove that right belief and strong community are essential.

Emphasis on the power of community is another theme of modern thought, running from Rousseau through socialism, nationalism, and Bagehot's cake of custom to contemporary radicalism and talk of the public sphere. There is, of course, nothing strange or particularly new in the assertion that true community is based on shared belief. When they invoke community, then, fundamentalists rely on a long tradition but also speak to a world well prepared to hear; and they make their call concrete and immediate through their emphasis on personal ties and communal activities. By insisting that right community and true individualism are consonant, fundamentalists find in religion a solution to one of the central dilemmas of modern thought, one that has proved difficult for liberals and socialists.

Nor do fundamentalists stand alone in their criticism of modern industrial society. No age has ever produced more or more powerful autocritiques; none has ever disseminated them so broadly. A modern adult need not be literate to have been affected by religious, romantic, Marxist, anticolonialist, or nationalist assessments of how the world has gone wrong. Fundamentalist leaders and a great many of their followers borrow effectively from this arsenal of censure. They preach to a society subverted.

All of this is highly self-conscious, and that too is very modern. Hegel was well aware that the burden of history is increased choice, and that in a sense has become the central topic of novels and theater, newspapers, and politics, as well as sermons. But religion has always been about choice, so fundamentalists can speak to the most modern of preoccupations, and they can do so in the powerful voice of theology and with the concrete specificity of advice columns and television talk shows. Although its message is different from that of Greenpeace, Amnesty International, or societies opposed to some specific cruelty, fundamentalism fits well into a world of organized movements concerned with moral and social choice.

Problems of social change also contribute to fundamentalism's modernity. The change most cited is secularization. Fundamentalists can enfold everything they oppose into that one rubric, whether or not they are aware that social scientists, not often so generous to fundamentalist self-assessment, tend to accept that opposition. Indeed, an older scholarly literature makes it necessary to add that secularization should not be too simply seen as a process inimical or external to religion. The secularization of society at large offers religion increased autonomy, and it has been encouraged by the desire for a religious life independent of the state, less tainted by politics, and freer of institutional and social compromise. The claim to that autonomy has become an important part of modern religion. Fundamentalism is not just a reaction to secularization but a product of it. Modern societies tend to establish a kind of equilibrium between this autonomy of religion and the demands of secular society. Fundamentalism tends to break down that equilibrium, in part as a consequence of the very independence secularization has conferred. Autonomous religious communities develop a kind of concentrated power, expanding from narrow definitions of religion's role to general family mores, to broader social relations, and to law, institutions, and culture. This can generate explosive forces as members of the religious community seek to extend their own coherent sense of meaning to more and more aspects of public behavior, reaching out into the secular society around them and crossing accepted lines of demarcation between recognized spheres, thereby upsetting the established balance. Fundamentalism's rising demands of the larger society are resisted by others as a violation of prior understandings and a threatening effort at domination. These efforts to tame, delimit, or control this expansion are experienced by fundamentalists as repression that necessitates resistance.

Other tendencies in modern society also ease the way for fundamentalism. Democratization and changes in social structure and culture, while making political leaders more sensitive to organized groups, have tended to weaken the position of established elites. Because their legitimacy now depends more on performance than on who they are and because social mobility allows newcomers access to posts of power, elites become less cohesive and more vulnerable to criticism. Both bureaucratization and ideological division undermine the sense of reciprocity that encourages compromise, a situation in which fundamentalists are comfortable. With the fervor of moralists, fundamentalists are quick with criticism and suspicious of compromise as the path to corruption. Modern institutions provide easy targets, modern society a ready audience.

Significantly, fundamentalists are likely to be especially effective in their criticisms of established religious institutions and leaders. Where such religious institutions exist in relative harmony with secular authority, they are denounced as compromised by that balance between the religious and secular that fundamentalists have come to challenge. Traditional leaders are suspect for blurring the distinctions between passionate believers and those who merely conform or are respectfully indifferent. Far readier than more conventional clerics to judge and to denounce, fundamentalists expose traditional religious leaders as hesitant compromisers, lacking in moral courage. In calling for reformations they invoke models and traditions of which every religion is proud (and lay claim to martyrs), while using the language of modern concerns and contemporary standards to lambaste the latitudinarian tendencies of institutional religion. What Max Weber labeled, a little distantly, as an emotional community of laity fits the late twentieth century as well as the sixteenth.

Fundamentalism also addresses the situation of the modern family, anointed in contemporary rhetoric, both secular and religious, which conceives the family as an achievement of personal choice, a model of social organization, and the locus of cultural values. Since the nineteenth century, demands from and expectations for the family have steadily risen. Divinely ordained and the base of society, it must also be the permanent center of love and an effective source of child rearing that lasts longer and longer. For two centuries social commentators have taken the condition of the family as the measure of social health, although during that time the family has changed in purpose, size, and economy and has been, or is said to have been, buffeted by a baffling array of additional changes that range from geographical mobility to altered sexual mores and shifting definitions of the rights of children and women. In focusing on the family, fundamentalists combine modern modes of thought with neuralgic sensitivity to modern social change. Their romanticized recollection of older patterns of paternalism and gender roles, like the collective past discovered by nationalists, addresses very modern concerns.

If fundamentalism is connected to many salient elements of modern history generally, it has also benefited from a number of developments characteristic of the period since World War II. Religious communities have become easier to establish. Contemporary politics around the world has taught effective techniques of recruitment and mobilization, and organization is less difficult in formally structured urban life. Fund-raising works better in cash economies and where people have more money; and fundamentalism is facilitated by the ease with which resources of money, information, and equipment can be transferred, as well as by the greater prosperity. Above all, mass communication has made an enormous difference. Radio, tape cassettes, and television are now accessible (in contrast to cinema, which is much more costly to produce, distribute, and display). Ideally suited to a propaganda of unproblematic theology neatly tied to the troubling news of the moment, these mass media have demonstrated the capacity to create a sense of shared community among people who have never seen each other and may not even have known they had much in common. The opportunities are quite literally almost unprecedented.

Fundamentalism may even have benefited from the effects of the cold war. In a world apparently divided on ideological lines, societies embraced ideologies and techniques that discriminated between friend and enemies, between loyalty and treachery; and these practices, which may have helped to legitimate a similar tenor in other movements, were congenial to fundamentalist certitude. Capitalist and communist parties not only taught the world the techniques of mass demonstrations, effective organization, and propaganda but showed how all public issues can be related to a basic schism. The understanding of crime, poverty, social conflict, or immorality became matters of ideology and measures of belief quite independently of fundamentalism; and dichotomous thinking became less alien and more respectable as it became more common among elites and in general discourse, offering fundamentalist arguments a more comfortable environment. The impact on fundamentalism of attitudes external to it shows strikingly in the surprising willingness of fundamentalists to recognize international affinities and inspiring examples across regional and national boundaries, though less easily across religious ones.

The political and social changes of the past half century have made issues of identity critical ones in most contemporary societies, clearly so in national liberation movements but evidenced as well in established polities. Everywhere, populist movements, demands for the recognition of ethnic groups (often newly defined), and conflicts over the rights and privileges to which they are entitled have presented new political opportunities while challenging old coalitions and established procedures. Establishing social identities entails the definition of boundaries and can build on distinctions of status, class, race, and geography. In all of this, religion is central, not only because systems of belief and communal rites are the core of social identity but because religion's transcendent concerns allow unmatched flexibility in the weight given to all other social distinctions. Thus, religious movements can appeal to differences of class and ethnicity or cut across them, even shifting emphases and in effect changing the demarcations themselves in midcourse. Students of nationalism have long since come to recognize creative inventions on which historic claims often rest, but since World War II cultural boundaries of every sort have been extraordinarily fluid. Again and again, political maps have been remade. Domestically, the very possibility of democratic political participation altered or eliminated the lines between those who are and are not included in public life, while social change altered distinctions of class. Vast movements of population suddenly put in juxtaposition groups that before had hardly needed to define their similarities with and differences from their neighbors. International markets and mass media created virtual neighbors suddenly.

It may be, of course, that the urge for some sort of religious fundamentalism is universal and present in all ages. An important change in the second half of the late twentieth century, then, would be that the barriers inhibiting development of such movements have been lowered. The enforcement powers of traditional religions have been eroded by secularization, constitutions, legal systems, and popular attitudes. Most governments have come to claim some indifference on matters of theology, and most societies have attempted some greater tolerance of religious diversity. In addition, there has been a broad, though hardly universal, tendency in the past thirty years and especially in the past decade, for states to favor some decentralization of political power and decision making, favoring a local autonomy that gives fundamentalism new opportunities. This distrust of centralized command, useful to any movement not in power, has been increased by the state's deeper penetration into society. A source of resentment, greater intrusiveness has also brought to the public agenda the very issues of personal conduct and social ethics central to the fundamentalist program. Ideas, social change, and technology have made it easier in the contemporary world to act independently of established institutions.

These global influences on fundamentalism go beyond the demonstration effects of similar movements elsewhere. Fundamentalism is likely to be stronger where convenient models are available to illustrate the evils of amoral development free of religious guidance. These negative models may be found in a prosperous neighbor or trading partner, but television images of the United States have undoubtedly been the most valuable of all. Like the negative view of crime-ridden and licentious New York that circulates in the American South, this sense of a destiny to be avoided carries particular weight in societies feeling the force of modernizing changes and the impact of increased contact with a larger world. The passionate warnings and clear prescriptions of fundamentalists offer a contrasting and welcome reassurance. In their analysis, the evils of that world can be avoided without rejecting all the advertised benefits of economic growth, democracy, and social harmony. Both promises of a brighter future and warnings about its current direction can borrow from the insights and rhetoric of the cultural criticism found in intellectual circles worldwide. The language of disdain and hope in existentialism, Marxism, anti-Marxism, anticapitalism, and antiimperialism is available to all.

The Local Situation

Because fundamentalist movements grow and prosper by integrating personal life with society and transcendent values, the history of any single movement is intimately connected with the society in which it operates — with local attitudes and values, social structure and tensions, institutions and politics. Perhaps, however, the points made so far can be brought together to say something about where fundamentalism is more likely to thrive—where, that is, there might be reason to expect modern religious movements incorporating some of the modes of thought and addressing some of the social issues characteristic of modern times and especially of the past fifty years.

1. The belief in change as a historical process, for example, may be more likely to become the focus of ambivalent attention (*a*) where patterns of change have long been observed but from a distance; (*b*) where ideologies of change have been widely promulgated, by a radical opposition or a reforming state and by prominent political figures, writers, military or business leaders, and the media; (*c*) where there has been recent local experience of very visible change; and (*d*) where those changes have had distinctively differential effects, creating new opportunities and careers for some, loss of jobs and opportunities for others, and placing added strains on traditional ties of family, kinship, and hierarchy.

2. The belief that change is a natural process with a direction of its own may be stronger where change is understood to be imposed from outside—the result of pressures from capitalist interests located elsewhere (much as midwestern progressives once viewed eastern banks and railroads), from colonial power, from the demands of technology, or from the messages carried by international mass media. The intrinsic tendencies attributed to this historical process can be expected to reflect prior experience of cultural encounters through colonialism, migration, and the media, and those expectations will be redefined by the local experience of economic development and urban growth.

3. The belief that human beings can reshape the process is likely to be greater where there has already been effective mass mobilization through religious, radical, democratizing, or nationalist movements and where ideologies of change have been widely promulgated, establishing a discourse that incorporates ideas of modernization, liberation, or Marxism. Of these, Marxism may paradoxically be the most influential for fundamentalism, not simply as a foreign threat to religion but as an explicit, systematic, and exclusive ideology that proclaims certain kinds of change to be universal and inevitable while at the same time controllable and potentially beneficial if properly directed—for fundamentalism, too, tends to incorporate these assumptions while contesting alternative interpretations, balancing belief in the efficacy of human agency with a useful emphasis on its limitations.

4. The belief that change is best controlled by building on community is likely to be greater (*a*) where concepts of community have recently come to be self-consciously defined (in terms of social relations, customs, dialect, food, and space); (*b*) where community is understood to extend beyond face-to-face contact, class or condition, and urban or rural residence;

and (*c*) where the principle of authority is thought to reside in community rather than inherited position or impersonal bureaucracy. To all of this, fundamentalism brings coherence and higher meaning, for the community it seeks is a community of belief. And it is empowering. The fundamentalist community appeals not simply to the marginal but to women, students, engineers, and entrepreneurs who feel they are treated as marginal, who are educated enough, energetic enough, hopeful enough, and individualistic enough to insist that their own lives must have purpose and to believe that they can create communities that will give them their rightful place and thereby remake society.

The practice of fundamentalist communities tends to flow along the local fault lines of politics and social organization and to coalesce around conflicts, from national wars to local schools. Conflict is so important because it reifies the boundaries that construct and define community. Fundamentalists need enemies, but their communities must be based on more than issues and must be or claim to be somewhat independent of economics or politics. So they seek to base community on a more stable similarity of habits and values. Distinctive rites, dress, and customs are taken to be the proper behavior that expresses belief. While demarking community, these also make that community accessible to others who are willing to adopt their ways, thereby demonstrating that mores are more than local anthropological accident. Although this capacity to invest local habit with transcendent significance has powerful appeal, analysts should not conclude that fundamentalist communities are simply defensive devices for protecting the old ways. It is shared behavior as an expression of higher purpose that matters, which is why these behavioral markers of community, though imported, serve just as well in the evangelical movements of Central America or Korea. A beleaguered group is not enough to produce fundamentalism, but it is more likely to flourish where social and political divisions are most easily susceptible to religious and ethical interpretations.

Community is thus more likely to be based on shared belief where extra-religious institutional expressions of it are weak, centered at a distance, or undergoing change and where organized religion has long been associated with a wide range of social activities and public rituals. Even where ethnic or regional identity is obviously very important to a fundamentalism's success, liturgical and other explicit markers of identity connected to beliefs are likely to be more prominent. Fundamentalism tends to prosper, in fact, where a collective package of mores once considered markers of community seems to be coming apart. It promises to place social ties on a different footing, something with poignant meaning, where families seem endangered by fathers and sons moving away to distant work, where networks of kinship and paternalism appear threatened by women's independence, where hierarchies of age and occupation could be bypassed through education, or where valued ways of life are called into question by rising awareness of attractive alternatives.

The fundamentalist community of belief often addresses real and possibly pressing problems that the established social system prefers to ignore or seems powerless to solve. In contemporary societies these issues are especially likely to be ones involving individual social behaviors—prostitution, selling and using drugs, domestic conflict, violent crime, illegitimacy, and abortion—widely understood to be both measures of moral health and effects of social change. For problems of this sort, no one offers clearer explanations and firmer prescriptions than fundamentalists.

If these propositions have some merit, they should also prove suggestive when applied to those societies in which many of the conditions favorable to fundamentalism exist yet vigorous fundamentalist movements have not emerged. Canada, Wales, and Germany since unification are cases in point. Canada has a strong and diverse Protestant tradition that includes many conservative churches, and it has a history of strong protest movements, yet fundamentalism there in no way matches its prominence in the United States. Could a missing element be absent or weakened optimism about the power of human agency to shape the historical process of change, which pours inexorably from the giant to the south? Wales, where identity is strong and strongly religious, where radical and nationalist protests have flourished for a century, sustained by biting unemployment and poverty, might be expected to produce the world's most musical fundamentalism. Could the failure to do so be related to both the continued dominance of England and to the feebleness of utopian ideologies there? Since unification, Germany has wrestled with ferocious issues of identity, economic dislocation, and disruptive change; these have fed ugly violence and intolerance but apparently not a modern fundamentalism. Could a partial explanation lie in the long absence of religious leaders from public life in eastern Germany, in the strength of secular institutions, and in the possibility that issues of social change, however unresolved, have been too familiar for too long to provoke fundamentalist answers?

Neither atavism nor aberration, fundamentalism is quite at home in the modern world it rarely likes. Its core remains the discovery in religious faith of clear, unproblematic rules for daily life and inspired guidance toward a better society. For scholars, God may be in the details, but fundamentalists find him in the local and ordinary.

The Effects of Fundamentalism

If fundamentalism partakes of the modern era, it also affects it. Its effects on politics, in society after society, are well known, although they differ case by case. But even where it may not reach so far, fundamentalism contributes to modern life as a counterweight to some tendencies and reinforcement of others. It helps to remind the world how much religion still matters and how warmly human beings respond to community, and it propounds a kind of moral equality no matter what the divisions of power, status, and class. It strengthens cross-generational bonds and sanctions resistance to social claims presented as irresistible, whether the argument for them is practical (society cannot prevent premarital sex, social harmony requires acceptance even of religious diversity) or moral (as in the arguments for gender equality, pluralism, and toleration). It heightens fears about the future but also optimism that it can be controlled.

Religious movements are as rich in irony as any other, and these effects are often not the ones intended. Fundamentalism is an important agent of change, altering politics and restructuring social division. By connecting community mores to the transcendental, fundamentalism justifies their vigorous defense and preservation; but in the process it transforms much of the flexible durability of custom into codified rules of behavior whose very explicitness almost inevitably guarantees that they will be subject to formal amendment. As vigorous modern movements, fundamentalisms absorb and use ideas and tactics drawn from the world at large, thus helping to domesticate within their communities influences that might otherwise seem alien in their newness. Assuring their members that mores are maintained by following rules, fundamentalisms ease adaptation where few rules apply. While codifying traditional values in order to preserve them, fundamentalisms adapt many of them and legitimate others quite new. Connecting specific behavior, through religion, to universal values permits using the rhetoric of universality in defense of local ways, at the same time injecting preoccupation with general cultural values into matters that might have been viewed as merely local and customary. Thus, local and particular behaviors and the ways of evaluating them become more intertwined with national and international ones. Religion's claim to the transcendental continues to stretch the community beyond its own confines.

Conclusions

As many have noted, few fundamentalists accept the term and fewer still acknowledge that their movement belongs in the same category with others to which we give that label. The perception of fundamentalism as a worldwide phenomenon is ours: the product of a Western, academic, and social scientific outlook rooted in a particular set of values that not only favors pluralism, tolerance, rational discourse, regular procedures for decision making and adjudication, openness, democracy, and universalism but that sees these qualities as favored by certain kinds of historical change. Fundamentalisms are perceived to have much in common because they seem to challenge and maybe seriously threaten these values. That is fair enough. It does not matter that the values we proclaim (themselves connected to religion in the minds of many) may contain contradictions, but it does matter how opponents of fundamentalism respond to its presence.

On the whole, studies of fundamentalism do seem to suggest that direct confrontation and therefore policies of repression (definitions of which will differ, however) are unwise. While bruising the values they may be meant to serve, such policies are likely to be counterproductive. Putting pressure on fundamentalists and giving them reasons to be fearful is likely, at least in the short run, to strengthen their internal cohesion, validate their own denunciation of the world around them, and strengthen the boundaries between them and Other on which they depend. Even when explicit pressure does reduce whatever immediate threat fundamentalism is thought to represent, it will have serious human, moral, and political costs.

If it is true that fundamentalism addresses real ethical, personal, and social problems, then the analysis fundamentalists present and the solutions they propose need to be listened to with an understanding and even sympathy that recognizes their concerns. Our challenge is to seek ways of meeting those concerns consonant with the values we hold. We need to hear the message of fundamentalism, including the human yearning it expresses, as readily as we judge its practices.

Note

1. Martin E. Marty and R. Scott Appleby, eds., *Fundamentalisms Observed* (Chicago: University of Chicago Press, 1991), *Fundamentalisms and the State: Remaking Polities, Economies, and Militance* (Chicago: University of Chicago Press, 1993), *Fundamentalisms and Society: Reclaiming the Sciences, the Family, and Education* (Chicago: University of Chicago Press, 1993), *Accounting for Fundamentalisms: The Dynamic Character of Movements* (Chicago: University of Chicago Press, 1994), and *Fundamentalisms Comprehended* (Chicago: University of Chicago Press, 1995).

⁛ 2 ⁛

Critical Issues in Arab Islamic Fundamentalism

Ziad Abu-Amr

Drawing on the cases of Egypt, Algeria, Jordan, Palestine, and the Sudan, this chapter defines and analyzes several aspects of the phenomenon of Islamic fundamentalism in the Arab world, such as the way the phenomenon is defined, the high profile it has assumed in recent years, the host of factors contributing to its rise, and the way Islam is presented as an alternative civil and political order. This study also provides some general remarks that characterize Islamic fundamentalist movements. In the conclusion the future prospects for Arab Islamic fundamentalism are assessed.

Definition

Perhaps no issue is more controversial in the study of Islamic fundamentalist movements than defining the phenomenon. Different parties tend to use different definitions that reflect their particular perspective and interest in the phenomenon. The term *fundamentalism* literally means "to go back to the fundamentals"; in the case of Islamic fundamentalism, "to go back to the fundamentals of Islam" means to restore the Islamic character to state and society. Arab Islamists[1] prefer to use the term *revivalism* because of the negative connotations of fundamentalism. In the opinion of this writer, *fundamentalism* is a neutral word, connotations notwithstanding. Some non-Islamists (Arab and foreign, Muslims and non-Muslims), on the other hand, tend to equate Islamic fundamentalism with negative concepts such as backwardness, fanaticism, militancy, and terrorism.

Such labels are usually politically motivated. The Muslim fundamentalists who fought the former communist regime in Afghanistan and were supported financially and politically by the West and its allies in the Middle

East, the Arab world, and elsewhere were called *mujahidin*, a favorable term meaning "freedom fighters engaged in a holy war." When some of these fundamentalists returned from Afghanistan to their own countries (Egypt, Algeria, Jordan) and opposed existing governments there, which are generally pro-Western, they were described as Islamic fundamentalists or even Islamic terrorists.[2] The double standards are obvious: the Islamists are classified according to where they stand vis-à-vis the other side and not based on firm commitments to and practice of doctrinal beliefs.

It becomes evident, therefore, that no simple definition of Islamic fundamentalism can enjoy consensus. This simple definition is not possible, according to John Voll, because Islamic fundamentalism is not a monolithic movement, and there is a wide diversity of individuals and groups associated with it.[3] Furthermore, according to James Piscatori, "many variants of Islamic fundamentalism exist," and thus one comprehensive, encompassing definition of the phenomenon is misleading.[4]

High Profile

The phenomenon of Islamic fundamentalism has captured the attention of the world. Several factors account for the high profile of the phenomenon. First, Islamic fundamentalism reflects the reality of an actual religious revival in Muslim societies in several parts of the world. Islam had not been absent from these societies, but the revival has led to a higher profile of Islam in Muslim politics and society.[5]

Second, the failure of ruling Arab elites to translate liberalism, socialism, and other secular ideologies into familiar local idioms, apply theory to practical needs, and solve major problems in their societies focused attention on Islam as an alternative. "Western-oriented policies of government and elites appeared to have failed," writes John Esposito. "Neither liberal nationalism nor Arab nationalism/socialism had fulfilled its promises."[6] Loss of faith in these secular ideologies was magnified by the collapse of socialism in the former USSR and East European countries.

Third, the stereotype and perception of Islam as a threat to Western interests and secular and liberal ideals have put the phenomenon of Islamic fundamentalism in the spotlight. The West tends to equate Islamic fundamentalism with destabilization and violence. If political Islam prevails in the Arab world, there is a fear that Western interests may be threatened. Islamic fundamentalism is also perceived as a threat to pro-Western Arab governments. The negative Western view of Islam, furthermore, is sometimes linked to historical tensions and hostility between Islam and Western Christianity, as epitomized in the Crusades.

Most Arab regimes find the phenomenon of Islamic fundamentalism threatening and subversive. It can be a threat not only to stability but also to the very legitimacy of these regimes, most of which are not democratically elected. Secular and liberal Arab individuals and groups join the governments in seeing Islamic fundamentalism as a symbol of backwardness and an impediment to development, progress, and freedom. On the other hand, a large segment in society sees in Islamic revival a mechanism for the desired change and salvation.

At least in part, Islamic fundamentalism is dramatized for political reasons. Certain governments (especially Israel) and political circles (in the Middle East region and elsewhere) wish to replace communism with Islamic fundamentalism as the major threat to Western interests in the region. Promoting such arguments would maintain or increase the strategic relevance of these governments and circles. Hence, the persistent publicity campaigns to demonize Islamic fundamentalism and the calls to combat it. The fact that Islamic fundamentalism is an internationalist movement with a totalitarian ideology invites a partial comparison with communism. The negative attitude of Islamic movements toward the new world order makes these movements liable to Western accusations. Muslim fundamentalists believe that after the collapse of communist regimes in the former USSR and Eastern Europe, Islam remains the only challenge and target to Western hegemony.

Finally, the tactics employed by some Islamic groups account for the high visibility Islamic fundamentalism has assumed. Attacks on Western and Israeli targets and highjackings and hostage taking in various parts of the world are automatically associated with Islamic fundamentalism as a whole. Indeed, some people consider violence to be a defining characteristic of Islamic fundamentalism. In reality, however, violence is not an essential characteristic of any political group, including the Muslim fundamentalist groups. The resort to violent tactics in Lebanon and Palestine against Israeli targets, for example, is shared by Islamists and non-Islamists alike. In Egypt and Algeria violence is an instrument not only of the Islamic groups but also of the governments. In Iran the Islamic revolution took place without resort to widespread political violence.

Causes

Observers posit various causes for the rise of Islamic fundamentalism in the Arab world. The causes fall into two broad categories: the first attributes the phenomenon primarily to external factors, especially Western challenges and threats. The fears and suspicions of Muslims, especially the

Islamists among them, are not a pose; they are genuine. Some of their fears are justified, but Islamists are oversensitive to what they perceive as a world conspiracy against Islam and the Muslims. In this sense Islamic fundamentalism may be seen as a cultural reaction to imported ideologies from the East and West (e.g., liberalism, modernism, and communism). Islamists and Muslims in general tend to associate elements of these ideologies with atheistic notions or with the corruption of society and moral values.

The second category attributes the rise of Islamic fundamentalism primarily to internal factors. Arab political systems have failed to build a public order that enjoys legitimacy; and subsequent Arab governments, as well as the spectrum of political elites, have failed to deliver and solve chronic problems in their societies after raising the expectations of their peoples. "The rise and proliferation of fundamentalist movements are thus related to the perception of a decline in legitimacy of the arbiters of Muslim opinion, whether these are the government, the *ulema* (learned religious men) or established reformist movements," writes Piscatori. "Unable or unwilling to redress perceived injustices and inequalities, political and religious elites, even sometimes existing Islamist movements, come ineluctably to bear the hallmarks of failure."[7]

The process of modernization, especially when it is equated with westernization, has alienated large segments of Arab populations. As with Marxist and liberal programs, the failure of the modernization process to solve the problems of Arab societies resulted in disillusionment. Piscatori rightly argues that the rise of fundamentalist Islam "is not so much a reaction to the failures of modernization, though that acute sense of disappointment is obviously present; but, rather, a reaction to the failures of leaders—religious as well as political—to deal with these failures."[8]

The natural tendency among Arab Muslims has been to seek an untried alternative. The failure of other ideologies and the resulting ideological vacuum have made Islam a natural choice for the faithful who dream of restoring a historical Islamic order and for the frustrated laymen who seek solace in their religion and tradition. Thus, in addition to the general external and internal categories that explain the rise of Islamic fundamentalism, one finds causes peculiar to specific Arab countries or contexts.

The renewal of doctrine is one of these indigenous causes: in recent years there has been a genuine interest in Islam as a faith and an increase in religious commitment to its teachings. This shift has provided a necessary context for the rise of Islamic fundamentalism, which emerges when people's religiosity begins to assume a political character. Both external and internal factors helped to release a religious aptitude among the Arab Muslims; the complex problems engulfing Arab societies made alienated Muslims prone to Islamic political rallying and recruitment.

The liberation of Palestine from Israeli occupation has been the most resilient issue to mobilize Islamic sentiments. Islamists perceive the loss of Palestine in 1948 and the establishment of a Jewish state in its place as an encroachment on Muslim land. Since its loss, Palestine has functioned as a catalyst and rallying point for Islamic revival. The Israeli occupation of Jerusalem and the occasional Israeli impingement on Muslim holy places in it, together with continued and extensive Jewish settlement of the city, inflames Muslim fundamentalist sentiments. Israel stirs Arab Muslims' fears. It is viewed as a spearhead of Western hegemony and an alien body in the heart of the Arab world. Western support to Israel adds fuel to Muslim fundamentalist fire. Israel, for its part, has reinforced this Muslim perception by its occupation of Arab lands and its frequent encroachments on its Arab neighbors.

Seeds of contemporary Arab Islamic fundamentalism can thus be found in the Arab-Israeli wars. The defeat of the Arabs in the 1967 war exposed the Arab Muslims to their weakness. Islamists attributed this weakness to failure in embracing Islam and applying its teachings and to resorting instead to failing secular ideologies. The defeat was "God's punishment on a people who had abandoned the straight path of Islam."[9] The Egyptian Muslim Brotherhood Society, for example, considered the defeat a "divine revenge" against the Gamal Abdul Nasser regime for its persecution of the Egyptian Brothers and for its failure to follow divine laws.[10]

The 1973 war, on the other hand, served to strengthen the religious climate in the Arab world, particularly in Egypt. The Egyptian "victory" in the war was attributed to the faith of the troops and the power of the doctrine: "In contrast to the Arab-Israeli war which was fought by Nasser in the name of Arab nationalism/socialism, this war was fought under the banner of Islam."[11] It was reported that Egyptian troops shouted, "Allahu akbar [God is great]" while crossing the Suez Canal.[12] Islamic groups used both the 1967 and 1973 wars to raise Islamic consciousness in the Arab region.

Although it is a tactic of Palestinian Islamic fundamentalists, the Intifada—the Palestinian popular uprising that began in late 1987—has given impetus to Arab Islamic fundamentalism as a whole. It enabled the Palestinian Islamic groups, Hamas and the Islamic Jihad, to engage the Israeli occupation and hence empower political Islam and Islamic fundamentalism as a whole. The role the Palestinian Islamic groups played during the Intifada was a source of admiration, inspiration, and mobilization for other Islamic groups in the Arab world. It projected political Islam in practice against a country that managed to defeat major Arab states. Israeli measures of collective punishment against the Palestinians and Israeli designs on Arab Jerusalem have heightened the Muslim fundamentalist sentiments and resentment.

Among the specific regional triggers for the rise of Islamic fundamen-

talism one must also acknowledge the role of the Iranian Islamic revolution. Indeed, the Islamic revolution of 1979 in Iran was perhaps the most
important factor in the rise of contemporary Islamic fundamentalism. This
revolution, which presented Islam in action and victorious against the
powerful regime of the shah of Iran, provided the Muslims and Islamists
elsewhere with a source of inspiration and a model to emulate. The revolution instigated political activism, militancy, and fundamentalism among '
other Islamic groups. Furthermore, since 1979 the revolutionary Islamic
regime in Iran has extended different forms of support to Islamic movements in the Arab region.

Socioeconomic hardships in Arab societies, manifested in poverty, unemployment, and illiteracy, also provide local and regional warrant for the
expansion of Islamic fundamentalism among large segments of the Arab
population. The two most dramatic cases where harsh socioeconomic conditions have played into the hands of Islamic fundamentalism are Egypt
and Algeria. Islamic fundamentalism in these two countries has provided
not only a protest ideology for an ever-expanding disenfranchised population but also a haven for the poor, who are unable to overcome their
problems in society and who are inclined to resort to an outside power, in
this case God and religion, for salvation. While the long-awaited expectations of these people have been frustrated by existing Arab governments,
many Islamic groups have extended social welfare services when government services have proved inept or inadequate to the task. The Islamic
Salvation Front (FIS) in Algeria and a variety of Islamic groups in Egypt
provided food, clothing, and temporary housing. Such activities helped
Islamists to attract adherents.[13]

Exclusion from political rule also ranks as a local cause of Islamism.
Despite the deep horizontal penetration of several Arab societies, such as
Egypt and Algeria, by Islamic groups, these groups have been denied up-
ward mobility, political participation in government, and legal status in
political life. In Algeria, for example, FIS was denied the fruit of its victory
in the parliamentary elections of 1991. In Egypt the Muslim Brotherhood
Society, which is the largest political opposition group in the country, has
been denied legalization. The case of Jordan is an exception. The Islamists
there have access to political power. Unlike Egypt and Algeria, Jordan has
made them an integral part of national politics. Due to the equal opportunity available to them, the main Islamic group in Jordan, the Muslim
Brotherhood Society, has not resorted to political violence.

The failure of reformist Islamic politics to bring the Islamists to power
has radicalized segments of these groups and pushed them to adopt violence to achieve their objectives. In Egypt small radical and violent groups
have split from the reformist Muslim Brotherhood, which failed after sev-

eral decades to seize power in the county. The result has been a state of polarization within the society regarding the appropriate tactics that should be used against the incumbent regimes. In Algeria, for example, the Islamic movement was radicalized and resorted to violence because it was denied the victory it scored in the parliamentary elections in the country.

Finally, government policies and measures toward the Islamists in some Arab countries have radicalized the Islamists and driven them toward violence. Instead of trying to solve the root causes that beget political violence, especially harsh socioeconomic conditions, both the Egyptian and Algerian governments have applied excessively harsh measures against the Islamists, a policy that was bound to draw violent reactions. Government efforts to deal with symptoms of the problem by violent means deprived these governments of widespread popular support. In both Egypt and Algeria, society seems to be indifferent to the struggle taking place between the Islamists and the regime.

Islam as an Alternative Political and Civil Order

Muslim fundamentalists see in Islam an alternative civil and political order to existing non-Islamic orders. In this regard the Muslim fundamentalists provide Islamic views regarding a host of major issues, such as state and society, political rule, pluralism and democracy, civil society, the new world order, and the Middle East peace process.

The traditional Islamic view presents Islam as both a religion and a system for life (*din wa dawla*). The Muslims have readily available laws, known collectively as the Shari'a, and interpretations of life and its various aspects. These laws and interpretations are derived from the Quran and the Sunna. But despite this traditional view, Islamists seem to be unable to agree on one specific model of Islam, a situation that creates diversity and confusion. In the Arab world today there are different models and brands of Islam. There is, for example, the Islam of Rashid Ghannoushi in Tunisia, and there is the Islam of Hasan al-Turabi in Sudan. Ghannaoushi's Renaissance Party is banned, whereas Turabi's National Islamic Front controls the government of Sudan. In addition to difference in articulations, the difference in political status is bound to affect the views of the two groups. The same can be said about the FIS in Algeria and the Islamic groups in Egypt, Jordan, and Palestine.

Needless to say, the state Sunni Islam of Saudi Arabia is radically different from the state Shi'a Islam of Iran. Both Islamic states have their Muslim detractors. The Islamists are discontent with the Islamic model of Saudi Arabia and with Islamic institutions patronized by incumbent regimes in the Arab world. This brand of Islam is usually described as the "Islam of the Court."

Diverse currents exist even within each Islamic movement: "This diversity extends to attitudes toward modernization, militancy, the West, democratization and pluralism, the role of women, etc."[14]

The issue of political rule is a primary concern for Muslim fundamentalist movements. It is an ultimate objective for these movements, although it is not always explicitly stated. Instead of bluntly talking about the seizure of political power, Islamic movements in the Arab world talk about the objective of establishing an Islamic order or polity (state and society). In the process of working toward that objective, Muslim fundamentalists have to make decisions regarding their participation in non-Islamic orders, the terms of this participation, and its forms.

The peculiar situation of Islamic groups in each Arab country defines the Muslim fundamentalist agenda regarding political rule. The Muslim Brotherhood societies in both Egypt and Jordan, for example, commit themselves to nonviolent Islamization of state and society. Therefore, they are willing to participate in the existing non-Islamic political orders of President Mubarak in Egypt and King Hussein in Jordan. This willingness to participate in political rule may be considered tactical or interim, since these movements hope to seize full power in the long run. On the other hand, the militant Islamic groups, al-Gama'at al-Islamiyya, refuse to deal with the regime of President Mubarak and seek violently to topple it. In Algeria, after being deprived of its victory in parliamentary elections, the FIS resorted to violence and spawned a radical militant wing, the Armed Islamic Group (GIA). In short, the Islamic agenda with regard to political rule is not uniform, and the tactics of the Islamic groups are in some cases defined by the incumbent political regimes.

Muslim fundamentalists object to the concept of democracy. They dismiss it as a secular Western concept and reject a governmental system emanating solely from the will of the people. The Islamic alternative to this concept is *shura*, an Islamic principle that has its roots in the Qur'an, the holy book of Allah. From an Islamic point of view, *shura* contains all the positive aspects of democracy and much more.[15]

Despite this general line of Islamic thinking, the Islamic attitude toward the concept of democracy is far from uniform. There is more than one Islamic discourse in this regard. There are those Islamists who totally reject the concept, arguing that when there is a text (the Qur'an) there is no place for legislation by man.[16] Other Islamists argue that democracy can be accepted as a transitional phase toward the implementation of the *shura*, but once Islam rules, there will be no room for non-Islamic concepts or practices. The appreciation of democracy in this sense is political and tactical since it can help the Islamists seize political power.

The Muslim Brotherhood societies in Jordan and Egypt and the FIS in Algeria embrace this attitude. Some Islamists, such as Rashid Ghannoushi of Tunisia and Hassan Turabi of Sudan, see no contradiction between Islam and the essence of democracy and argue that the two may be reconciled. Ghannoushi does not call for democracy as it is practiced in the West because he believes that the Western practice of democracy is undemocratic and hypocritical. Ghannoushi favors democracy by default; he argues that, in the absence of an Islamic order, Western democracy remains the best system. Finally, Ghannoushi argues for adopting the democratic idea but only after revising it to become consistent with the spirit of Islam. While he also supports pluralism, human rights, freedom of expression and belief, participation in political life, and rotation of power through the ballot box and while he rejects violence to solve political and ideological differences among citizens, he wants to free the Western concept of democracy from the polluting elements of secularism and nationalism.[17]

Ghannoushi's discourse is eclectic and may be described as heretical by traditional Islamic schools, which argue that fixed and sacred religious principles or teachings cannot be mixed or confused with man-made concepts. In this sense, Ghannoushi is seen to be arbitrarily reconciling the irreconcilable, since the source of authority and legislation in democratic nations is the people, whereas the source of authority and legislation in an Islamic state is the word of God as inscribed in the Qur'an. Turabi too is uneasy about linking democracy to secularism, and he is rather vague about the concept. He tends to equate democracy with populism or mass movements. In this sense he defines democracy in a way that suits his own purpose. He advocates tolerance, openness, and reform of Islamic thought in order to provide answers and solutions to modern problems.[18] On the other hand and as a reflection of confusing democracy with pluralism, Turabi would allow pluralism but does not address the issue of circulation of power to groups that do not embrace Islam as a frame of reference. The right to circulation of power to all citizens is a major pillar of democracy.

Why do Islamists entertain a talk about the concept of democracy when it contradicts their doctrine? The following reasons may account for this attitude: first, many Islamists accept a pluralism and democracy while they are not in political power because a context of pluralism and democracy provides them with the freedom to mobilize, organize, and spread their ideas. Second, Islamists pay lip service to the concept of democracy to defuse internal and external pressure and accusations of being rigid, fundamentalist, and undemocratic. In a time in which democracy is the model, the Islamists do not want to be singled out or seem out of sync with a world trend. Third, Islamic interest in democracy may emanate from an epistemological break or confusion by the Islamic proponents of the concept. It may also emanate from a genuine belief that democracy and Islam are reconcilable. Islamic thinkers such as Ghannoushi and Turabi have been adequately exposed to the Western intellectual tradition. Turabi, for example, received his higher education at the Sorbonne and Oxford University.

Islamists view "civil society" with suspicion, together with other Western concepts such as pluralism and democracy. These concepts are perceived as part of Western ideological, political, and cultural penetration of Muslim societies. The concept of civil society also contradicts Islamic prescriptions. It presupposes a dichotomy between state and society. In an Islamic order both state and society are guided by Islam, not by any positive or mundane laws.

Nevertheless, despite the difference in the point of departure, there are certain similarities between an Islamic society and a civil society. The role of civil society organizations toward the state is undertaken by certain Islamic institutions—the "institutions of the umma"—such as the *ulema*, the mosque, the *waqf* (religious endowments), and the like.[19] The treatment of the state in Islam is common, but what is novel to the Islamists is the concept of civil society. Despite their objections to that concept and in addition to establishing their own institutions, the Muslim fundamentalists in several Arab countries have engaged in the activities of civil society organizations. They have established political parties (and participated in elections) and voluntary social, educational, and professional organizations. This engagement is not an endorsement of civil society. Rather, it is only a means to penetrate society, Islamize it, dominate it, and seize power.

In their discourse the Islamists use the term "new world order" but in a critical and condemning fashion. To the Islamic political movements in the Arab world the emerging new world order is aggressive and hostile to Islam and the Muslims. The Islamists believe that after the collapse of communist regimes in the former USSR and Eastern Europe, Islam remains the only major challenge to—and hence the target of—Western hegemony. The Islamists, for example, refer to the war against Iraq, to Western double standards, to support for pro-Western regimes, and to the war against the Bosnian Muslims as manifestations of Western schemes against Islam and the Muslims. According to the Islamists, the unipolar new world order is bound to serve the interest of the United States, its Western allies, and Israel.[20]

Arab Muslim fundamentalists are likewise opposed to a peace process that would leave Israel intact. To these fundamentalists, Israel has no right to exist in Palestine, which is a *waqf* land to the Muslims. Therefore, Muslim fundamentalists are opposed to the peace agreements with Israel, and they condemn the Palestine Liberation Organization (PLO) and other Arab governments that have concluded or are trying to conclude peace agreements with Israel. Arab Islamists see in peace agreements with Israel a concession of Muslim Palestine to the "Jews" and a means to help Israel consolidate its hegemony over the Arabs.

Arab Muslim fundamentalists cannot match their declared position toward Israel and the peace process with deeds. They are aware of their limitations and are handicapped by the circumstances under which they live in their own countries. Some of these groups are reformist in their approach, as is the case with the Muslim Brotherhood in Egypt and Jordan. Other groups are preoccupied with their own fights, as is the case with the FIS in Algeria and the Islamic militant groups in Egypt. In the words of one Egyptian Brotherhood leader, liberating Palestine requires the mobilization of the entire Muslim nation. Given the existing conditions of Muslim societies and Islamic fundamentalist groups, this objective is far from obtainable, at least in the foreseeable future.

General Characteristics

Several features characterize Islamic fundamentalist movements and the fundamentalist phenomenon as a whole. First, the movement is modern in spirit and orientation. Decades ago, Islamic fundamentalism was not as visible and vocal as it is now; it was dormant or overshadowed by other predominant ideologies (nationalism, pan-Arabism, socialism, and Marxism) or suppressed by powerful and perhaps more legitimate political regimes. Prior to the rise of current Islamic fundamentalism, Islam assumed a religious and social rather than a political character. Currently, however, it penetrates several Arab societies and assumes a pervasive character.

Modernization is perceived as a major factor in the resurgence of Islam in Muslim societies, and most scholars consider Islamic fundamentalism to be a product of modern times, a modern phenomenon.[21] Islamic fundamentalist movements are informed about and engaged with the issues that are debated in modern societies (political rule, pluralism, democracy, etc.) and have their own views on these issues. While the media may represent or misrepresent the fundamentalists, the new breed of leaders and activists is articulate, informed, and very conscious of the media and the role it can play.

Second, Islamic fundamentalist movements are not homogeneous. They are diverse and linked to the peculiar conditions and circumstances of the societies in which they exist. In Egypt, for example, there is a brand of Islam that is reformist (the Muslim Brotherhood Society), but there is another brand of Islam that is radical and involved in violence against the regime (the Gama'at Islamiyya). In Jordan the Muslim fundamentalists are sharing power with a non-Islamist monarch. In Algeria, Islam is currently in the battlefield fighting for political power. In Palestine the Islamists are engaged in a struggle for national liberation against a foreign occupation and at the same time practice oppositional politics against the Palestinian national authority in the autonomous area in Gaza and the West Bank. In Sudan, Islam is in power and is going through a time of severe testing.

Muslim fundamentalist movements, third, are political movements that embrace Islam as an ideology. Therefore, it is natural that these movements would use the power of religion to serve political purposes. In many cases, these movements give the imperatives of politics precedence over the imperatives of the doctrine. In other cases the doctrine is manipulated to provide justification and legitimacy for certain political acts. This manipulation of doctrine is not peculiar to the Islam of the court but also includes Islamic political movements. The Muslim Brotherhood Society in Jordan, for example, devised religious decrees (*fatwas*) to justify participation in the non-Islamic government of King Hussein.

"In a sense, all Islamic movements are engaged in the quest for political influence," writes Piscatori. "The entire rationale of their existence is to change the society in which Muslims live so that they may more faithfully follow the dictates of Islam. A distinction is often asserted between those activists who seek to change society directly through political, possibly violent, means, and those who hope to do so gradually and indirectly by concentrating first on the content of individual Muslim hearts."[22]

Because Islamic fundamentalist movements are political, they are also pragmatic, taking into consideration prospects for gains and losses. Such movements calculate their moves carefully. They will draw on doctrine to justify their political choices and tactics, depending on the prevailing circumstances. If violent tactics do not serve a political purpose, the fundamentalists will not resort to them. Despite their pragmatic use of religion the Islamists claim the high moral ground. They resort to militancy or violence, according to them, when it is imposed on them and only as a last resort. This has been the argument advanced by the FIS in Algeria. Hamas in Palestine is committed to violence against Israel because, as the movement argues, this is the kind of language the occupier speaks and understands. But Hamas is also committed to nonviolent opposition to the Palestinian authority in the Palestinian autonomous areas, as long as the latter does not resort to violence against Hamas. In Egypt the Muslim Brotherhood Society does not resort to violence but is usually reluctant to condemn the violent tactics employed by the militant Islamic groups because the brotherhood has grievances against the government and its policies and the violent measures it undertakes against the Islamists.

In addition to these four characteristics of Islamic fundamentalist movements—that they are modern, heterogeneous, political, and pragmatic—one must also note that they are representative of significant numbers of the population. In the cases drawn upon in this study (Egypt, Sudan, Algeria, Jordan, Palestine) religion is not politically expressed by marginal or fringe groups in society but rather by major political movements with very sizable mainstream followings—people from the various social strata.

In Sudan, for example, where the Islamists are in power, they control all spheres in society. In Algeria, religion was until recently expressed by a majority group, the FIS, as indicated by the 1991 parliamentary elections in which the FIS won 82 percent of the popular vote. In both Jordan and Egypt, religion is expressed by the single largest and most organized opposition political group in society, the Muslim Brotherhood. On the other hand, the Egyptian militant groups that are engaged in violence against the government represent a radical trend whose size and following are not known. Despite the assumption that these groups represent a minority movement, they have demonstrated a considerable measure of resilience in facing a government with large coercive capabilities. Worth mentioning in this regard is the neutral stand of large segments of the Egyptian society in the struggle between these groups and the regime of President Mubarak. As for Hamas in Palestine, it is considered the second largest political group and the most serious rival to the nationalist Fatah movement, the main faction in the PLO, in the struggle to dominate society, define its direction, and assume leadership.

Sixth, current Islamic fundamentalist movements are conscious of the strength of nationalism. Therefore, they address the issue for its political significance but only within the broader Islamic frame of reference. The Islamists are aware that the majority of the Arabs, regardless of whether they observe the outward manifestations of religion or not, insist that they were born and remain Muslims. Under certain circumstances or in response to certain challenges, Islamic underpinnings in the consciousness of the Arab automatically surface. Muslim fundamentalists have relied on such underpinnings in their attempts to mobilize support.

Islam has been an important factor in defining the relationship of the Arabs to the rest of the world. Arab secularists who are opposed to fundamentalism jump to the defense of Islam when fundamentalists are criticized or attacked by non-Arabs. The return to Islam can be seen as a search for identity in the face of what is perceived as foreign encroachments or hegemony.

Seventh, fundamentalisms have deep psychological roots. Regardless of the social class and historical experience of each fundamentalist movement, there is a shared sense of religion as a haven, a shelter against internal and external threats. Religion also provides solace in time of stress. Religion can appeal to the poor, the rich, and the elite. The poor seek religion either as an object for salvation or as a protest ideology. For the rich and the elite, religion can provide a spiritual, moral, epistemological, or intellectual frame of reference.

Islamic fundamentalists also rely heavily on slogans and generalities but are quite weak on the specifics of political and social reform. "Theoretical or ideological statements are often not accompanied by specific models for change," Esposito notes. "Islamic movements tend to be more specific about what they are against than what they are for."[23] Islamic discourse, for example, talks about "the Islamic state" and "the Islamic society," but it does not address specific dimensions of these concepts or the mechanisms of their implementations. Islamic discourse also talks about "the Islamic solution" and "the Islamization of knowledge" without identifying the components of these slogans. Furthermore, current Islamic discourse suffers from ambiguities when it comes to critical issues such as pluralism, democracy, human rights, the rights of women, the rights of minorities, and the like. When it tries to address such issues, Islamic discourse becomes incoherent and eclectic and loses its Islamic purity.

Instead, Islamic discourse focuses on ethics and moral values. It depicts the crisis of contemporary Arab Muslim societies as a crisis of ethics and moral values. It does not pay much attention, except only superficially, to the complicated problems facing societies worldwide, such problems as the distribution of wealth, food shortages, pollution of the environment, and the arms race.

Finally, a tenth characteristic of contemporary Islamist movements is their tendency to blame others for the ills of the Arab world. Their discourse repeatedly points to the failure of Western and Eastern ideals and ideologies (capitalism, liberalism, communism, nationalism, etc.) in delivering Arab and Muslim societies from poverty. Muslim fundamentalists also tend to blame others—national governments or foreign powers—for the failures of the Islamists themselves. Islamic discourse places the Islamists outside the state of crisis and deterioration from which other ideologies and ideas and the governments that embrace them suffer.

Islamic fundamentalists thus present Islam as the only alternative to these ideologies and ideas. In Islamic discourse the call to return to Islam as an alternative comes as a result of the failure of other alternatives, not because Islam has entered the contest and objectively proved to be the successful alternative model. In presenting their case, Islamists focus on the glorious past and the promising future. The present time is described as a period of trial (*mihna*). Islamic discourse has been preoccupied with the formulation of responses to accusations leveled at Islam and the Muslims, namely, that they are rigid, metaphysical, irrational, oppressive, antidemocratic, and violent. Because of this preoccupation, Islamic fundamentalism has not given much attention to creative thinking or to the initiation of programmatic solutions to standing and pressing problems.

Conclusion

Islamic fundamentalism is no longer a transient phenomenon. It may rise or decline, but it is not likely to fade away in the foreseeable future. Preoccupied with internal or domestic problems and concerns, Arab Islamic movements are evolving into nation-state political movements, at the expense of the pan-Islamic call, or pan-Islamic nature of these movements. In the past many people thought it was a wave that was bound to subside. The high tide of this wave was the Iranian Islamic revolution and its aftermath. But while the Islamic revolution itself subsided and attempts to export it receded, Islamic fundamentalism has gradually been institutionalized. It has become an integral part of the existing reality in several Arab societies and has been linked to major issues and problems in these societies. Esposito argues: "Viewing Islam and events in the Muslim world primarily through the prism of violence and terrorism has resulted in a failure to see the breadth and depth of contemporary Islam. In particular, many have overlooked the quiet revolution that has occurred in many parts of the Muslim world, the institutionalization of Islamic revivalism. . . . Islamic revivalism is no longer a movement of the marginalized few; it has become an institutionalized part of mainstream Muslim life."[24]

The institutionalization of Islamic fundamentalism has manifested itself in a number of spheres. It has become an ideology and has created its own political and intellectual discourse. The phenomenon has also created its own norms, means, and institutions. Therefore, it has become difficult to dismantle the phenomenon. It may rise or decline, but it is not likely to fade.

Furthermore, Islamic fundamentalism has become able to regenerate itself. Although Muslim fundamentalist movements provide an alternative vision to the existing situation in Arab societies, these movements usually thrive on the various and ongoing societal crises that incumbent governments have failed to solve. While not in political power, these movements grow, and their influence expands often by default, that is, not necessarily because of any tangible achievements they have offered to society but because of the failure of the others to do so.

Therefore, the future success or failure of Muslim fundamentalist movements hinges, to a great extent, on the ability of existing governments to deliver and solve chronic political, social, economic, cultural, and psychological problems. It also hinges on the ability of these governments to mobilize coercive capabilities to violently suppress the Islamists.

So far, and as a general trend, there are no adequate indicators to assume that the influence of Muslim fundamentalist movements is subsiding, although it sometimes seems that this influence is stabilized or receding. The series of suicide attacks carried out by Hamas and the Islamic Jihad against Israeli targets in January and February 1996 indicates a rise in the level of Islamic violence. Likewise, the violent attacks against American troop installations in Saudi Arabia in 1996 are indications of a rise in radical Islamic fundamentalism in that country.

In Algeria the incumbent government is unable to solve the critical problems of the country and is equally unable to suppress the Islamists. On the other hand, while the Islamists have established their turf, they have not been able to topple the government after five years of violent conflict with it. In Egypt, despite existing poverty and other economic and social problems and despite the continuing violent attacks of Islamic militants, the government still enjoys adequate capabilities to combat these militants and to neutralize the mainstream Muslim Brotherhood Society.

In Jordan the engagement of the Islamists in national politics through parliament and party life has provided them with additional avenues of access. Their rejection of political violence is not proving to be a liability in terms of maintaining or even expanding their existing influence. In Palestine the Islamists continue to capitalize on the nationalist problem. The Israeli occupation of some Palestinian territory continues to exist, and the peace agreement between Israel and the PLO is not yielding the desired outcome. A majority of the Palestinians are also anxious about the future of the peace process.

In assessing the future prospects for success and failure of Muslim fundamentalist movements, one cannot ignore the role external factors can play. It is not likely that Israel would stay neutral, for example, if Hamas should prevail over the PLO in Palestine or that they even would allow this eventuality to materialize without attempting to prevent it. The same can be said about a potential Islamic takeover in Jordan or Egypt. Egypt in particular is extremely significant for the strategic interests of Israel and Western countries, especially the United States. If Egypt falls to the Islamists, other countries in the region are likely to follow. Therefore, foreign powers are not likely to be discrete or timid about intervention, in one form or another, although the desired outcome of such intervention cannot be guaranteed.

Finally, the Islamic alternative cannot be tested until the Islamic order is established. In this sense, the example of the Sudan is significant to Islamists and non-Islamists alike, although the Sudanese Islamists claim that their model is not yet complete.[25] But if the Islamists fail in their enterprise, they may argue that they have tried and that what is destined by God is destined. An Islamic mind-set is predisposed to this kind of justification. This mind-set would even credit the Islamist for the sheer act of trying.

Notes

1. It is necessary to make a distinction between Muslims and Islamists. The Muslims are those who follow the faith of Islam but do not necessarily wish to live under the Islamic Shari'a rule in an Islamic society, while the Islamists are those Muslims who strive to live in an Islamic state and society modeled along the state and society established by the prophet Muhammad and his companions.

2. Western countries and media, especially in the United States, label Islamists who work against friendly governments as Muslim militants or terrorists. Israel describes the Hamas activists who wage attacks against Israeli targets as terrorists. And the Egyptian government refers to Islamists who attack police forces as terrorists; the same is done by the Algerian government.

3. John O. Voll, "Fundamentalism in the Sunni Arab World: Egypt and the Sudan," in *Fundamentalisms Observed*, ed. Martin E. Marty and R. Scott Appleby (Chicago: University of Chicago Press, 1991), pp. 345–402.

4. James Piscatori, "Accounting for Islamic Fundamentalism," in *Accounting for Fundamentalisms: The Dynamic Character of Movements*, ed. Martin E. Marty and R. Scott Appleby (Chicago: University of Chicago Press, 1994), pp. 361–73.

5. John L. Esposito, *The Islamic Threat: Myth or Reality* (New York and Oxford: Oxford University Press, 1993), p. 11.

6. Ibid., pp. 14, 15. 7. Piscatori, "Accounting," p. 363.
8. Ibid., p. 361. 9. Voll, "Fundamentalism," p. 376.

10. Ziad Abu-Amr, *Islamic Fundamentalism in the West Bank and Gaza: Muslim Brotherhood and the Islamic Jihad* (Bloomington: Indiana University Press, 1994), p. 11.

11. Esposito, *Islamic Threat*, p. 17.

12. Abu-Amr, *Islamic Fundamentalism*, p. 11.

13. Piscatori, "Accounting," p. 365.

14. Esposito, *Islamic Threat*, p. 167.

15. Ziad Abu-Amr, "Palestinian Islamists, Pluralism and Democracy," in *Democracy, Peace, and the Israeli-Palestinian Conflict*, ed. Edy Kaufman, Shukri B. Abed, and Robert L. Rothstein (Boulder, Colo.: Lynne Rienner, 1993), p. 247.

16. Ibid., p. 249.

17. George Giacaman, "Democracy at the End of the Twentieth Century," in

Burhan, *About the Democratic Option: Critical Studies*, ed. Burhan Ghalyun et al. (Beirut: Markaz Dirasat al-Wahda al-Arabiyya, 1994), pp. 37–38 (Arabic).

18. Ibid., p. 37.

19. For a methodological review of the Islamic view of civil society, see Seif Eddin Abdul-Fattah Ismail, "Civil Society and the State in Contemporary Islamic Thought and Practice" in *Civil Society in the Arab World*, ed. Said Bensaed al-Alawi et al. (Beirut: Markav Dirasat al-Wahda al-Arabiyya, 1992) (Arabic).

20. For two influential Islamic views on the new world order, see Fathi Yakin, *The International Variables and the Required Islamic Role* (Beirut: Mu'assasat al-Risala, 1993) (Arabic), and Munir Shafiq, *The New World Order and the Confrontation Alternative* (Nablus: Al-Nashir, 1992) (Arabic).

21. Esposito, *Islamic Threat*, p. 11.   22. Piscatori, "Accounting," p. 368.

23. Esposito, *Islamic Threat*, p. 164.   24. Ibid., p. 199.

25. For an elaborate discussion by Hassan Turabi of this issue and other matters relevant to the Sudanese Islamic example, see Arthur L. Lowrie, ed., *Islam, Democracy, the State and the West: A Round Table with Dr. Hassan Turabi* (Tampa, Fla.: The World and Islam Studies Enterprise, 1993).

ː 3 ː

Religion, Ethnicity, and Nationalism in India

T. N. Madan

Two dramatic incidents, each involving serious damage to or destruction of a place of worship in north India and loss of human life, highlight the explosive character of religious nationalism in our times. In each case the damaged or destroyed place of worship was sacred to a religious minority. While the destruction in one case came at the hands of violent mobs drawn from the majority Hindu community, the perpetrator of violence and vandalism in the other case was, ironically, the secular state.

On the evening of 5 June 1984, a carefully selected regiment of the Indian army moved toward the Golden Temple complex in the city of Amritsar in Punjab. It had orders of the Union (federal) government to "flush out" armed Sikh extremists along with their leader, a politically motivated fundamentalist preacher called Jarnail Singh Bhindranwale, from the Akal Takht ("throne of the immortal God"), the second temple comprising the complex, and some adjacent buildings. The Akal Takht had been converted into a fortress by Bhindranwale's followers, including a former, experienced Sikh general of the Indian army dismissed from the service on charges of corruption.

The occupation and fortification of the Akal Takht by militants violated well-established conventions associated with sacred places of worship. The Shiromani Gurdwara Prabandhak Committee (SGPC) and various Sikh political parties (the Akali Dals) were responsible for the maintenance of Sikh temples (called *gurdwara*, "abode of the Guru, that is God"). Although the SGPC and the Akali Dal were pledged to protect the sanctity of the *gurdwara*, they did not prevent or protest the sacrilege committed by Bhindranwale and his followers. Thus, they became accomplices in the blatant use of temples—places of worship—as arenas of conflict.

The three generals in charge of the operation in a hierarchical chain of command included two Sikhs. They were asked to use "minimum force" and to avoid "if possible" any damage to the main temple, the Harmandar Sahab ("the honored temple of God") and to minimize damage to the Akal Takht. The Harmandar Sahab, also called the Golden Temple because of its golden canopy, has long been considered the holiest of all Sikh *gurdwaras*.[1] In a significant statement to the press later, one of the generals overseeing the operation, himself a devout Sikh, declared that "the Indian army is a religious army." The senior general (a Hindu) confirmed this and elaborated in another press statement: "We went inside with humility in our hearts and prayers on our lips. We in the army hold all places of religion in equal reverence."[2]

Nonetheless, the infantry-type operation turned out to be longer, tougher, and bloodier than the generals had reckoned. By the morning of 6 June reinforcements were called in after the army suffered heavy casualties and the militants remained barricaded inside the Akal Takht. Finally, a tank was sent into the complex, leading to the near destruction of the Akal Takht. Bhindranwale, his followers, and quite a few pilgrims—6 June was an important Sikh religious holiday—died in the operation. The number of those killed was perhaps three to four times the five hundred acknowledged by the government. Many of those inside the complex surrendered to the army or made good their escape or hid themselves. When the obviously distressed president of the republic of India, a Sikh of humble origins who had grown up to become a clever politician (the Indian presidency is modeled on the British constitutional monarchy), visited the temple complex a couple of days later, militant snipers in some uncleared buildings were still not entirely vanquished.

Both the antagonists in the violent confrontation—namely, the Sikh community and the Indian government—emerged with their reputations badly damaged from the operation (code-named Blue Star). More than a dozen years later, the wounds have still not healed.

The Indian state is secular by self-definition. The constitution of India opens with a declaration to this effect in the preamble. It also contains detailed provisions in the chapter on fundamental rights and elsewhere, forbidding the involvement of the state in the religious affairs of the citizens in a discriminatory manner, except when public order, morality, or health are deemed to be in jeopardy. The secularism of the state is usually defined in India as "equal respect for all religions" (*sarva dharma sambhava*), rather than in terms of a "wall of separation" between the sacred and secular domains. The Union government's decision to use military force to free the Golden Temple complex of elements that it considered antisecular, antinational, and secessionist was not a pious act to end the sacrilegious occupation of the sacred precincts of the holiest of Sikh *gurd-*

waras, although some politicians did not hesitate to assert that this indeed was the case. The decision to use the military was political; the objective was to end the challenge to the authority of the secular state within its internationally recognized territory, a challenge mounted by religious fundamentalists and the purveyors of communal, secessionist politics.

In the eyes of the government and its supporters, who included many Sikhs from all walks of life, Bhindranwale and the Akali politicians represented a fusion of religious fundamentalism and religious nationalism, whose ultimate objective was the establishment of a separate, religious state. According to the official ideology, the only relevant identity in the political arena is that of the individual as citizen. Collective identities of race, gender, language, and religion, although significant in other contexts, are of no concern to the state, except insofar as affirmative action may be necessary to protect minority interests. While the secular state considers the citizenry to be homogeneous with regard to the application of the federal constitution, it supports cultural pluralism in its various manifestations, including the religious.

In the eyes of the militants, however, the Indian state was ungodly in its official ideology and biased in favor of the Hindus in practice. In his speeches to Sikh audiences, for example, Bhindranwale dwelled on the theme of the enemies of the Sikh faith, whom he identified as fallen Sikhs, hostile Hindus, and the atheistic state.

Sixty to 80 percent of the population of India is Hindu (the precise figure depends on whether the so-called Scheduled Castes and Scheduled Tribes are excluded from or included with the Hindus). Sikhs account for only about 2 percent. Numerically, the Muslim community stands between the Hindus and the Sikhs (Indian Christians at 2.5 percent are a marginally larger community than the Sikhs) and constitute over 12 percent of the population. Thus, it may not be surprising that the second of the two dramatic incidents of violent religious nationalism that I mentioned at the outset involved a Muslim mosque (*masjid*, "the place for making religious bows").

Just as Amritsar is considered a holy city by the Sikhs, Ayodhya in Uttar Pradesh is so regarded by the Hindus. For the believers among them, Ayodhya is a city of most ancient (in fact mythic) times, where Vishnu (one of the gods of the Hindu trinity) took human form as Rama, an avatar and exemplar of righteous conduct. According to the oral tradition, temples had been built or rebuilt from time to time to mark *Rama janma bhumi*, that is, "the place where Rama was born" of his human mother. The tradition also maintains, but without clinching evidence, that such a Rama temple was demolished in 1528 by a general of the conquering Muslim king Babar (founder of the great Mughal dynasty of India). The general then constructed a mosque in its place to commemorate his master's victory. It came to be known as Babar's mosque (Babri Masjid). Although the local king was a Muslim, the collapse of his kingdom was perhaps of lesser consequence to his Hindu subjects than the desecration of the temple, but there were no major altercations between the Hindus and the Muslims as a result of it.

The first recorded bloody communal riot occurred in 1853–1855, shortly before the native state of Avadh was annexed by the British. Mindful of the imperative of peace in the acquired territories, the new rulers made arrangements for the Hindus to worship on a raised platform outside the mosque, while the Muslims were provided protection to say their prayers inside, as indeed they had been doing for over three centuries.

India became free, and Pakistan was born as a result of the partition of the subcontinent in 1947 on the basis of religious difference. The birth of the two new states was accompanied by widespread, violent communal disturbances, followed by the movement of millions of refugees in either direction, Hindus and Sikhs fleeing from Pakistan and Muslims from India. The government of the United Provinces (now called the state of Uttar Pradesh) in India thought it prudent to declare the inner area of the Babri mosque out of bounds for both the religious communities, and the gate leading into it was locked. This put an end to praying by the Muslims, but the Hindus could still perform their rituals of devotion outside the building. Two years later (in 1949) some Hindus managed to break into the mosque and placed a stone image of the infant Rama (*ram-lalla*) inside to proclaim that he was born where the mosque now stands. The locks were put in place again, but the image was not removed for fear of a violent Hindu reaction.

In 1984 a Hindu right-wing cultural and political body, the VHP (Vishva Hindu Parishad [World Council of Hindus]),[3] initiated a campaign for opening the mosque so that rituals could be performed inside. As a prelude to calls for the destruction of the mosque this propaganda campaign gathered public support among the Hindu population, and the district authorities agreed in February 1986 to open the mosque.

As expected, the Muslim response was one of widespread and at times violent protest. The Hindu right wing closed its ranks in counterreaction, and the VHP, the BJP (Bhartiya Janata Party [Indian Peoples Party]), and the RSS (Rashtriya Swayamsevak Sangh [National Assembly of Volunteers])[4] adopted the construction of a "grand" Rama temple at "the birthplace of Rama" as their common objective. The foundation stone of such a structure was laid in 1989 at some distance from the mosque, but the widely publicized plans and models of the temple showed clearly that its sanctum sanctorum would be located where the mosque stood. Further steps by the VHP–BJP–RSS alliance to proceed with temple construction resulted in a clash with the state police in 1990, and about two dozen Hindu volunteers lost their lives.

National and state elections in 1991 gave an electoral boost to the BJP, however, and the party was able to strengthen its position substantially in the national parliament and form the government in four states, including Uttar Pradesh. This paved the way for the eventual destruction of the Babri mosque. From late summer onward, after BJP had assumed office, the expectation (or fear) that the mosque would be destroyed was widespread. It assumed the character of a national concern, and the Union government was consumed by the problem, trying to find a via media between the intransigent Hindu right wing and an equally stubborn Muslim leadership. The latter believed (not unreasonably) that if it agreed to the demolition, the way would be opened for more mosques in various north Indian cities, associated with the assertion of Muslim domination in medieval times, to be torn down. The state government and the BJP leadership gave formal assurances, including to the Supreme Court of India, that ceremonies planned for 6 December 1992, to give an opportunity to "pilgrims" from all over India to contribute voluntarily and symbolically to the "sacred" task of the construction of the temple, would be peaceful.

Thousands of Hindus, most of them apparently in a defiant mood, and the senior leaders of the VHP–BJP–RSS alliance were in Ayodhya by 5 December. More people were pouring in. Fearing the worst, most Muslim residents of the city, who had not experienced a communal riot in a long time, escaped to the safety of other places. Photographs published later showed that a group of Hindu militants conducted a rehearsal of the demolition, obviously with the knowledge of the civil authorities and the police. On 6 December the Hindu political leaders made fiery speeches, while those with a relatively sober image just looked on or made themselves scarce. The frenzied crowds, armed with crowbars, hammers, and the like, destroyed the domes of the mosque; the falling masonry was instrumental in destroying the walls. Within a few hours, the Babri mosque was rubble.

The prime minister of India, who had trusted the Hindu leaders, said that the nation had been betrayed. He promised that the mosque would be rebuilt (presumably by the government) and ordered dismissal of BJP governments in all four states in which they had come to power the previous year. Some communal organizations, including the RSS, were banned a few days later. The Supreme Court upheld the dismissals, proclaiming once again that secularism was an unalterable feature of the Indian state.

(It may be noted here that in 1984 there was no state government in Punjab at the time of Operation Blue Star as the same had been dismissed by the Union government for its alleged inability to contain Sikh militancy.)

The frenzied mobs that had participated in or jubilantly witnessed the destruction of the mosque went on a rampage in Ayodhya the next day, destroying or looting Muslim homes and businesses and killing some one dozen Muslims who had not left the city. Communal riots in many towns and cities all over India followed, leaving several thousand (mostly Muslims) dead and much property destroyed. In a final act of retaliation, criminal elements among Muslims in the premier western city of Bombay bombed it in March 1993, causing loss of life and property.

The impact of the events in Ayodhya was widespread, as had been the repercussions of Amritsar, where more people had died (in Operation Blue Star). The chain of reaction in 1984 had cost the lives of Indira Gandhi, the prime minister, and several thousand Sikhs, who were killed in Delhi by Hindu mobs following Mrs. Gandhi's assassination by her Sikh bodyguards.

Amritsar had been the battleground for the confrontation of secular and religious nationalisms, the former represented in principle, although only imperfectly in practice, by the government of India, and the latter by Sikh extremists. The Ayodhya scenario was significantly different in form but similar to the earlier encounter in substance. The right-wing Hindu politicocultural organizations, backed by the BJP government in Uttar Pradesh, explicitly (indeed, defiantly) represented religious nationalism. Their most obvious opponents were various ad hoc Muslim groups, such as the Babri Masjid Action Committee (BMAC) that had been established in 1984–1985 and enjoyed varying degrees of support from several political parties. Together they represented the principle of the religious freedom of minorities (in fact of all citizens) and their cultural rights under a secular constitution. Not all of these groups or parties were themselves secular in character; instead, they adhered to the position of minority exclusivism or communalism in the political arena. As in Amritsar, so in Ayodhya: the Union government projected itself as the instrument and supreme symbol of the secular state, but the Muslims and their non-Muslim supporters accused it of indecisiveness and inaction and an unjustifiable willingness to believe the word of Hindu "holy men" and BJP politicians. Indeed, the severest form of criticism focused on the prime minister personally, who was (I think unfairly) accused of being an accomplice of the Hindu extremists.

In sum, secular, religious, and ethnic forces play significant roles in the confrontations and disputes associated with nationalism in contemporary

India. To comprehend the present significance of these forces it is necessary to reflect briefly on key aspects of India's modern history.

Hindu Revivalism in the Nineteenth Century

The last quarter of the nineteenth century was witness to the emergence of new linkages between religion and politics in India. In Calcutta, the seat of the British government of India and home of one of three modern universities that had been recently established, tradition-minded Hindus were learning to cope with the challenges posed by their modernist countrymen. Partly in retreat from the efforts of reformers, such as Rammohan Roy (1772–1833), the founder of the Brahmo Samaj (Society of God), to produce a new religious synthesis from the encounter of Vedantic (or Great Tradition) Hinduism and Protestant Christianity,[5] they yielded to a new religious enthusiasm centered on the worship of a supreme mother-goddess (Shakti, literally "Power").[6] Politically sensitive intellectuals translated this religious idea into the mystical concept of the country as the divine mother.

Bankimchandra Chatterji (1838–1894), one of the most accomplished intellectuals of his time, wrote a major novel, *Ananda Math* (1882), about patriotism. Grateful for what he considered its beneficial effects, Roy had prayed for the continuance of the British presence in India, but Chatterji wanted the end of foreign domination. He was convinced that the political subjugation of the country was a result of a degenerate Hinduism and a disunited Hindu society. First the Muslim invaders and then the Western powers had taken advantage of these failings. The purification of Hinduism and reformation of Hindu society were, therefore, the essential first steps toward national independence.[7]

Chatterji's concept of a rejuvenated Hinduism was different from Roy's religious syncretism in its appeal to an exclusive and reinterpreted Hindu past. His joining of religion and politics was not a strategy or device but a basic philosophical position: everything Hindu was ultimately merged into the Hindu religion. While Roy had stressed the regrettable indifference of the Hindus to other religions, notably Christianity and Islam, Chatterji deplored the Hindu indifference to history, which had resulted in its distortion by foreigners. In his considered view, nationalism without a sense of history was impossible. Similar ideas were put forward by other intellectuals in different parts of the country.

Rejuvenation of Hinduism and Hindu society and opposition to foreign cultural and political domination found a particularly uncompromising spokesman in Dayananda Sarasvati (1824–1883), a Hindu renunciant from western India, who established the Arya Samaj (Society of the Noble People) in Bombay in 1875. It was in Punjab in the north that the Arya Samaj achieved its most spectacular success in the field of religious and social reform: purification of Hinduism through a rejection of idolatry and ritualism and return to the original sources and regeneration of Hindu society through a repudiation of caste prejudices and uplift of women. Dayananda was no simple revivalist; in fact, he was an innovator and introduced the notion of readmission of non-Hindus (Muslim, Christian, and Sikh converts) to Hinduism.

The background to this movement of reconversion through purification and education was largely political. Not only had Punjab been longer under Muslim domination than the areas east and south of it, acquiring a considerable Muslim population through conversion and immigration, it had also become the focus of feverish missionary activity after the annexation of the province by the British in the middle of the nineteenth century. In no other part of India had British rule been so closely identified with Christianity as in Punjab, and nowhere had the support of the soldier and the administrator for the missionary been as explicit.[8] A crusade against Christianity was, in Dayananda's judgment, an essential component of patriotism; without a reassertion of Hindu identity, nationalism would remain only a feeble effort. Dayananda studied the texts and oral traditions of the major religions of India with the intention of highlighting their "errors." His *Satyarth Prakash* (The Light of Truth [1875]), a book of principles and precepts of social and religious life addressed to the Hindus, included a discussion of "the science of government." More than half of the book is devoted to highly intemperate criticisms of other religions. Needless to add, his prejudices far outweighed his knowledge.[9]

Nationalism and Communalisms

Regional socioreligious reform movements were active throughout the second half of the nineteenth century, more among the Hindus than the other religious communities of India. Implicitly or explicitly, these movements had political implications if not agendas too. A political organization at the national (all-India) level, namely, the Indian National Congress, was established in 1885 by a group of urban elites drawn from several religious communities, including a retired British civil servant. Its goals were moderate, if somewhat vague, and included the promotion of a "fuller development and consolidation" of "sentiments of national unity." In today's idiom, it had a secular agenda.

The representative character of the Congress was questioned, however, from the very beginning by certain Muslim leaders, most notably the educationist Sayyid Ahmad Khan (1817–1898) of north India. Although he had been a firm believer in the culturally composite character of sociocultural life in north India, Khan considered the objectives of the Congress inimical to the interests of the educationally backward Muslims. He wanted his coreligionists to benefit from the new economic opportunities that direct British rule was opening, of which the better-educated Hindus had been quick to take advantage. To achieve this, they needed time and British patronage. Moreover, he was distrustful of the introduction of local self-government and the mechanism of elections. He feared that the Hindus would totally override the interests of the much smaller Muslim community. Accordingly, Khan resisted the efforts of the third president of the Congress, Badruddin Tyabji, who was also a Muslim (from Bombay), to win his support for the Congress. On his part, Tyabji expressed the hope that there was nothing in the mutual relations of the different religious communities of India that would make any one of them refrain from joining with the others "to obtain those great general reforms" and "rights" that were "for the common benefit." [10]

Sayyid Ahmad Khan's fears were shared by many Muslim leaders. In the protection of the interests of their community, they founded the Muslim League, a political body, in 1906 as an adjunct of the Muhammadan Educational Conference. The latter organization had been created by Khan soon after the establishment of the Congress had been announced (in 1885). One of the first demands of the League was to ask for separate electorates in local-level elections, which were the only elections then held, so that the Muslims would choose their representatives and the Hindus theirs on communal lines. The ideology of communalism, according to which nationhood is defined primarily in religiously exclusive terms and only secondarily in territorial terms was thus introduced into Indian politics.

The basic premise of communalism was (and is) that the political interests of a religious community are unaffected by ethnic, linguistic, class, or any other divisions within the community. Rather, these interests are defined antagonistically in relation to other similarly conceived religious communities. Internal differences such as those along the lines of class cleavage were considered more manageable, and their resolution was held over for a later day. Religiously neutral secular nationalism and communalism (i.e., religious nationalism) thus emerged as rival ideologies. The secular nationalists regarded themselves as engaged in a struggle to end colonial domination, and considered religious, ethnic, and other similar differences of secondary importance, if not unreal. The communalists, in contrast, maintained that the fight against colonialism could not be joined unless the postindependence political and economic rights of religious minorities were first made secure.

It is important to note here that, in the communalist rhetoric, religion appears as ideology rather than faith. As Louis Dumont puts it, "Communalism, on the one hand, differs from nationalism in the place that religion seems to play in it, while on the other, the religious element that enters into its composition seems to be but the shadow of religion, i.e., religion taken not as the essence and guide of life in all spheres, but only as a sign of the distinction of one human, at least virtually political, group against others." [11]

While the politics of Muslim separatism was being spelled out, the Congress, although a predominantly (but not exclusively) Hindu body, maintained its secular stance, but this came to be defined more and more in religious-pluralist rather than areligious terms. And this spelled mischief. Hindu nationalists at the turn of the century proclaimed nationalism a divinely inspired religion. This was, needless to stress, an ideological construction, and it raised the question of the Hindu, Muslim, or any other source of inspiration. In spite of its secular program the Congress had to address the question of communal difference, and it tried to do so in a pluralist, inclusive manner. It recognized a hierarchy of interest groups but opposed subnationalisms unless included in the framework of mainstream secular nationalism.

In this context Mahatma Gandhi (1869–1948), at the beginning of his political career in India (after his triumphal return from South Africa in 1915), espoused the cause of the distant Ottoman sultan, who claimed the status of the caliph. Gandhi made this cause a component of his noncooperation movement directed against British rule because Indian Muslims were concerned about it. At first, Gandhi seemed to have worked a miracle: Muslim participation in the Congress and its programs reached unprecedented heights. But the abolition of the caliphate in 1924 by the secular Turkish nationalists brought the Hindu-Muslim collaboration to a quick end.

Hindu-Muslim hostility resurfaced with greater intensity. The communal ideology of *Hindutva*, or Hindu identity, which is currently enjoying an enormous vogue, was put forward, and an apparently nonpolitical cultural organization, the Rashtriya Swayamsevak Sangh (RSS), was established in the early 1920s. [12] Hindutva promulgated a restrictive definition of Indian identity in terms of the merger of the notions of "native land" and "holy land." This meant that those whose most holy lands are outside India (namely, Jews, Christians, and Muslims) were likely to be treated as "foreigners" and even denied citizenship rights unless they merged with the Hindu cultural mainstream. A totalizing concept of "national culture" was put forward; it denied the pluralism that had been promoted over the decades by the Congress as the specific character of Indian nationalism, rooted in Indian history and indeed in the Hindu religious tradition itself.

While secularism as religious pluralism was the dominant mode of thinking within the Congress, men like Jawaharlal Nehru (1889–1964) among its top leaders were secularists in the Western, Enlightenment sense of the term. Nehru had been deeply influenced by British socialist thinkers and by Marxism-Leninism. From the 1920s onward, up to the eve of the partition, he consistently denied that nationalism had any legitimate connection with religious identities. The most important thing, Nehru maintained, was the problem of feudal or class exploitation. In fact, it was more important than the problem of national independence. Echoing Lenin, he asserted that the question of religion was at best a "side-issue" and should not be allowed to occupy the front rank in the national movement. He considered national independence a prerequisite to the reordering of socioeconomic relations in society. Once such a reconstruction was done, Nehru was convinced, religious differences would retreat into the privacy of individual lives.

Although he was very close to Gandhi, the latter's mixing of politics and religion seemed utterly wrong-headed to Nehru; he did, however, acknowledge the importance of spiritual values in human life. As things turned out, Nehru's faith in the primacy of an economic approach to nationalism remained a minority (though strongly articulated) viewpoint within the national movement and had a severe setback when the country was partitioned in 1947 on the basis of the so-called theory of the religious communities of Hindus and Muslims as two separate, mutually exclusive nations. Nehru agreed to partition as a desperate measure. It is likely that he expected the partition to be undone by the economic forces that freedom would release.

As was expected, India gave itself a republican and secular state, while Pakistan decided to call itself an Islamic state, contrary to the wishes of its founder, M. A. Jinnah (d. 1948), who conceived of it, rather paradoxically, as a modern secular state. Even before the economic forces that Nehru expected the state to release in India had a chance to have an impact, subnationalisms of various kinds surfaced in India. And it is to these that I now turn.

The Tide of Cultural and Ethnic Nationalisms

The partition of India in 1947 on the basis of religiocultural differences was far from a complete solution to the clash of multiple identities and subnationalisms. The Muslim majority areas of the northeast and north-west were constituted into Muslim homelands (east and west Pakistan) and, potentially, an Islamic state. In the months after partition several million Muslims left their homes in India to migrate to Pakistan. About 40 percent of the one hundred million Muslims of the subcontinent remained in India, scattered over most parts of the country. They were no longer in a majority in any state except Jammu and Kashmir.

These Muslims decided, out of conviction or necessity, to dissociate themselves from the ideology of religious nationalism. For the limited purpose of the preferred form of government, they gave their support to India's being declared a secular state, but many among them did not embrace the broader ideology of secularism as a worldview. In the years following partition, the ideology of communalism (or religious nationalism) seemed to wane in India. Religion as the principal marker of collective identities was replaced by language. In Pakistan this became a critical issue almost immediately. The declaration of Urdu, the mother tongue of migrants from north India who had been in the vanguard of the demand for partition, as the official language was deeply resented by the Bengali-speaking east Pakistanis, who constituted more than half the population of the new state. West Pakistan comprised half a dozen speech communities, including the Urdu-speaking Mohajirs ("refugees"). The agitation against Urdu resulted in the recognition of Bengali as the second official language of Pakistan.

In the following years, Bengali ethnic nationalism emerged as a powerful force, recognizing racial, cultural, and linguistic differences and combining resentment against cultural arrogance and economic exploitation. Pakistan finally split into two states in 1971. The Bengali language had emerged as a key marker of ethnic identity. A switching of masks had occurred: in 1947, Bengali Muslims had identified with other Muslims of the subcontinent as *Muslims* who happened to be Bengalis; in 1971 they seemed to stress that they were Muslim *Bengalis* with a distinctive culture and the credentials to be an independent state. Since the achievement of that status, Bangladesh, which had declared itself a secular state (of the Indian type) at the time of its birth, has been witness to a resurgence of religion in public life and even the emergence of Islamic fundamentalism. The Bengali case is an excellent example of the dialectic of ethnic and national boundaries in contemporary South Asia.[13]

In India, cultural nationalism surfaced in the postindependence period in the form of two critical questions: the identification of an official state language and the reorganization of the constituent states of the union to make each coincide with a cultural region, with a particular language as its key symbol. Of the fifteen major languages of India recognized as such in the constitution and employing several scripts, Hindi had the largest number of speakers (currently about 30 percent of total population), but these were confined to four or five north Indian states. A mixture of Hindi and Urdu, called Hindustani, had been closely associated with the Congress (and the British Indian army) and was widely understood in urban areas outside the Hindi states. The adoption of Hindi as the national language was, however, opposed by the non-Hindi states, particularly those of the Dravidian areas of south India.

As a compromise, Hindi and English, the latter a colonial legacy, were both given the status of official languages, but use of English was to be discontinued after fifteen years. Meanwhile, efforts were to be made to promote the knowledge of Hindi. Since support for Hindi in the non-Hindi states was still very weak in 1965, the terminal year for the two-language formula, the existing arrangement was continued. Additionally, it was agreed that Hindi would not be imposed on any state not wishing to use it, and no deadlines would be set. These assurances were written into the constitution two years later, bringing the curtain down on an explosive issue in the context of nation-building. Complaints of Hindi (and north Indian) domination are, however, still voiced from time to time in the south.[14]

The second expression of cultural or ethnic nationalism in the post-independence years was the demand for linguistic states in place of the provinces created by the British, without following any consistent criteria but reflecting the prevailing situation of the colonial period. Government leaders, most notably the prime minister (Jawaharlal Nehru) and the deputy prime minister (Vallabhbhai Patel), opposed this demand, for both were supporters of a strong union, and linguistic reorganization represented a decentralizing tendency. Secular nationalism had imbibed some of the values of imperialism, such as the emphasis on centralized power. Moreover, for Nehru and modernists like him, primordial identities of any kind, religious or linguistic, could not be made the basis of the structure of a modern state.

The pressure behind the demand, representing the aspirations of large regional or ethnic formations, was enormous, however. Supporters and opponents of monolinguistic states reached a compromise by the mid-1950s, and in 1956 the Parliament agreed to a countrywide redrawing of internal boundaries. Certain safeguards were put in place: language was not to be used as a cover for religion and secession (as indeed was being done in the bilingual state of Punjab), and all the major linguistic communities concerned had to agree to the redrawing of boundaries. The process was completed only ten years later, when Punjab too was divided in a rather controversial manner.[15]

The manner in which the centrifugal forces were handled during the

1950s and early 1960s (under Nehru's prime ministership) clearly showed that, in a country as geographically vast and culturally diverse as India, centralization of power and a policy of *integration* were less likely to succeed than decentralization of power and a strategy of *accommodation*. The state had to be seen as providing a framework for the articulation of cultural and ethnic identities rather than as their suppressor.[16]

I have used the terms *ethnic* and *cultural* interchangeably and in relation to identities and subnationalisms within a federal political structure. Moreover, I pointed out that language (or mother tongue) is often used as a key symbol (or diagnostic feature) of a broader sense of cultural distinctiveness. Strictly speaking, the notion of ethnic identity implies valorization of real or putative (more often the latter than the former) common descent. The latter is linked to the idea of a shared cultural heritage, which is communicated and learned through a particular language.[17] Yet common descent—the sense of belonging to a single physical stock—is not an easily sustained notion in the case of large, multimillion-strong societies such as the speech communities of South Asia (whether the Bengalis of Bangladesh, the Tamils of India, or the Sinhalese of Sri Lanka). Among smaller communities, however, belief in common descent could be a significant factor in the emergence of ethnic subnationalism.

Among the areas in India where the concept of the nation-state and the legitimacy of national integration have come under severe strain, the border areas of the northeast adjacent to Bangladesh, China, and Myanmar have been prominent. Here well-known and large tribal communities (the so-called Scheduled Tribes) have struggled for a greater control over their affairs and even for secession in some cases (the Nagas and the Mizos). Over the years all the major ethnic groups of the region have won statehood within the Union of India. The overall approach of the Union government has been one of accommodation. The problem of aggressive ethnicity has not been wholly overcome in this area or elsewhere in the country. In fact, the Jharkhand area of the state of Bihar, home of many tribal groups (of Indo-Australoid racial stock and Mundaric linguistic affinity), is currently the scene of a political movement for separate statehood within the union. The most difficult case today is that of Kashmiri religious and ethnic nationalisms in view of their international ramifications.

When the British finally decided to wind up their colonial empire in South Asia, the so-called native states, which had acknowledged British paramountcy, were expected to "accede to" (join) India or Pakistan, keeping in view mainly the geographical and demographic (Hind-Muslim ratios) considerations. The state of Jammu and Kashmir in the north, having common borders with India and Pakistan (and China and the

USSR), was preponderantly Muslim but had a Hindu maharaja. The state comprised several cultural regions, including the predominantly Hindu Jammu province, the predominantly Buddhist Ladakh province, and the almost exclusively Muslim Kashmir province (the famed valley of Kashmir). The largest and most active political party of the state was the secular, socialist Kashmir National Conference, whose leadership and membership were largely Muslim. The conference had close ties with the Indian National Congress and during the 1940s repudiated the theory of two nations (Hindus versus Muslims) that was the basis of the demand for Pakistan.

While the maharaja hesitated, the newly formed Pakistan tried to seize the valley by force, using Muslim volunteers (of tribal origin from the northwest frontier) as a front. The maharaja, with the backing of the Kashmir National Conference, acceded to India in October 1947. In view of the abnormal circumstances then prevailing, necessitating military action by the government of India to drive out the invaders, the accession was accepted provisionally, to be ratified later through a plebiscite. Besides, the Indian government sought the intervention of the United Nations to clear the state of the Pakistani presence, which obviously was illegal. Nearly half a century later, the state of Jammu and Kashmir is still a subject of international dispute, and the valley has been the theater of a violent secessionist movement since the late 1980s. What is involved, besides various issues in the domain of international law and diplomacy, is the clash of secular, religious, and ethnic nationalisms.

The refusal of the Kashmir National Conference under the leadership of Sheikh Abdullah (1905–1985) to acknowledge the theory of two nations or to support the Pakistani claim to Kashmir as a Muslim majority area was not a unanimous Kashmiri Muslim decision.[18] The rival Kashmir Muslim Conference, although with a smaller following, was a supporter of religious nationalism. Once the maharaja had joined the Indian Union, with Abdullah's concurrence, Kashmir became an asset to it as evidence of its multireligious, secular character.

With the passage of time, however, strains developed in the relations between the Union and the state, mainly centered on the degree of autonomy the latter would enjoy. Article 370 of the Indian constitution bestows a special status on the state, but its content has been eroded over time through a series of agreements between a succession of federal and state governments. The relations between the Union and Kashmir are now virtually the same as prevail between it and the other states. This has generated resentment in some circles, which condemn the National Conference leaders as stooges of the Union. Moreover, the state has lagged behind in diversified economic development. As agriculture flourished in Punjab, tourism has done so in Kashmir, but industrial development has been tardy in both states, inviting charges of discrimination against the Union.

The early 1980s saw the rise of Islamic fundamentalism in Kashmir under the aegis of Jamaat-i-Islami and other fundamentalist organizations. They all derived inspiration from the Iranian revolution and generally supported the inclusion of Kashmir in the Islamic state of Pakistan. These groups have received material, moral, and political support from Pakistan. They have been opposed by the secular nationalist parties, whose numbers have multiplied but whose following has declined and who consider Kashmir a part of the Indian republic.

A further crucial development has been the emergence of the Jammu-Kashmir Liberation Front, which speaks in the name of the right of self-determination and asks for independence for the state. A vocal group among the seekers of independence, it emphasizes the ethnic distinctiveness of the Kashmir valley, pointing to a common physical stock (long noticed by anthropologists), a common language, and shared customs and practices. More significantly, the group claims that Kashmiri Muslims and Hindus are culturally different from the Muslims and Hindus of the rest of the subcontinent. These ideas are encapsulated in the notion of *Kashmiriyat*, or Kashmiri identity.[19] This carefully chosen word does not belong to the Kashmiri language; it has been borrowed from Punjabi and came into currency only in the late 1970s. As is recognized by the theorists of ethnicity, ethnic groups are fluid constructions, not permanently fixed or primordially given entities. They are "imagined" just as "nations" are.[20]

The religious composition of the population of the Kashmir valley, according to the 1981 census, showed a heavy Muslim preponderance (95 percent). The upsurge of an armed secessionist movement in 1989–1990 resulted in virtually all members of the Hindu minority fleeing the valley. In their absence, Kashmir is almost exclusively Muslim, and Kashmiriyat has a strong Muslim denotation. Indeed, some intellectuals have defined Kashmiriyat as "unceasing Islamization."[21] Consequently, religious and ethnic nationalisms merge and stand in opposition to a culturally pluralist secular nationalism.

Concluding Remarks

India is a storehouse of cultural and ethnic diversities; it has ever been so. Soon after it started on its career as a modern state, following partition on the basis of religious differences, many observers boldly predicted its disintegration because of the prevalence of many varieties of divisiveness (not mere diversities) emanating from religion, caste, tribe, language, region.[22] Fifteen years later, finding the country still intact and "developing a many-sided political form to match the baffling irregularity of her Daedalian social and cultural structure," Clifford Geertz admitted being confronted with "something of an Eastern mystery."[23]

Today, half a century after independence, India appears to have coped successfully with many of the challenges to her viability as a modern state. The apparent contradictions of the principles of liberal democracy, under which all individuals enjoy equal rights as citizens, and the caste system, which stands for institutionalized inequality legitimized by religious values, seem to have been overcome. The caste system has shown remarkable adaptability, and caste lobbies survive as vote banks. The Indian democracy is not a replica of Western democracies, but it works vigorously. Nor is caste today what it used to be; when caste groups and federations participate in competitive politics, they are secularized and function like ethnic groups.[24] Linguistic diversities too have been accommodated in a reorganized federal structure. Gradual decentralization of power and the growth of regional political parties have made it impossible for the Union government to impose from the top any language on unwilling states. The tribal communities also are gradually winning an increasing share in the socioeconomic development and self-governance of their traditional habitats, but several struggles are still raging.

The one major unresolved problem that remains is the relationship of religion and politics. Desecrated or destroyed places of worship have become one of its key symbols.[25] The rise of religious fundamentalisms and nationalisms to a peak in the 1980s made the task of resolution more urgent and much more difficult.

The Kashmir problem is the symbol of the unresolved conflict of communal loyalties and secular politics. Pakistani governments, one after another, characterize it as "the unfinished business of partition," by which they mean that, in view of its Muslim majority, the state and certainly the valley should belong to Pakistan. Independent international agencies (including the U.S. State Department) have confirmed that Pakistani governments have given support to terrorist groups in Punjab and Kashmir. While a minority of Kashmiri Muslims support the Pakistani position, the Indian government and the people generally remain committed to secular nationalism and the secular state.

But the situation seems to be changing. Since 1989 the Hindu right-wing BJP has enjoyed a string of electoral successes (and some failures, too). It emerged as a very strong political force in the 1996 parliamentary elections but with less than one-third of the popular vote. The BJP asked for the end of a special status for the Kashmir state and of what it calls "pseudo-secularism" or "the appeasement of religious minorities," particularly the Muslims.

For their part, large sections of the Muslim and Sikh communities point to the upsurge of Hindu fundamentalism and the destruction of Akal Takht and Babri Masjid as evidence of the inability of the secular state to protect the interests and places of worship of the religious minorities. Caught in a vicious circle of reaction and counterreaction, Hindu, Muslim, and Sikh communalisms, reinforced by fundamentalist ideologies and organizations, today pose a serious threat to secular nationalism in India.[26] A British political scientist, W. H. Morris-Jones, once observed that it seems to be the fate of India to invite forecasts of doom and then prove them wrong. He has been proved right in the past and, one hopes, he will be proved right in the future.

Notes

1. T. N. Madan, "The Double-Edged Sword: Fundamentalism and the Sikh Religious Tradition," in *Fundamentalisms Observed*, ed. Martin E. Marty and R. Scott Appleby (Chicago: University of Chicago Press, 1991), pp. 594–627.

2. Mark Tully and Satish Jacob, *Amritsar: Mrs. Gandhi's Last Battle* (New Delhi: Rupa, 1985), pp. 157–58.

3. Peter van der Veer, "Hindu Nationalism and the Discourse of Modernity: The Vishwa Hindu Parishad," in *Accounting for Fundamentalisms: The Dynamic Character of Movements*, ed. Martin E. Marty and R. Scott Appleby (Chicago: University of Chicago Press, 1994), pp. 653–668.

4. Ainslee T. Embree, "The Function of the Rashtriya Swayamsevak Sangh: To Define the Nation," in *Accounting for Fundamentalisms*, ed. Martin E. Marty and R. Scott Appleby (Chicago: University of Chicago Press, 1994), pp. 617–52.

5. V. C. Joshi, ed., *Rammohan Roy and the Process of Modernization of India* (New Delhi: Vikas, 1975).

6. See Christopher Isherwood, *Ramakrishna and His Disciples* (Calcutta: Advaita Ashram, 1965), and Amiya P. Sen, *Hindu Revivalism in Bengal c. 1857–1905* (Delhi: Oxford University Press, 1992).

7. See Sudipta Kaviraj, *The Unhappy Consciousness: Bankimchandra Chattopadhyay and Nationalist Discourse in India* (Delhi: Oxford University Press, 1995).

8. See Kenneth Jones, *Arya Dharm: Hindu Consciousness in Nineteenth Century Punjab* (Berkeley: University of California Press, 1976), pp. 6–13.

9. Ibid.; Daniel Gold, "Organized Hinduisms: From Vedic Truth to Hindu Nationalism," in *Fundamentalisms Observed*, ed. Martin E. Marty and R. Scott Appleby (Chicago: University of Chicago Press, 1991), 531–93.

10. See Shan Muhammad, *Sir Syed Ahmad Khan: A Political Biography* (Meerut: Meenakshi Prakashan).

11. Lois Dumont, "Nationalism and Communalism," *Contributions to Indian Sociology* 7 (1964): 48.

12. Ainslee T. Embree, "The Function of the Rashtriya Swayamsevak Sangh:

To Define the Nation," in *Accounting for Fundamentalisms*, ed. Martin E. Marty and R. Scott Appleby (Chicago: University of Chicago, 1994), p. 621.

13. See Mumtaz Ahmad, "Islamic Fundamentalism in South Asia," in *Fundamentalisms Observed*, ed. Martin E. Marty and R. Scott Appleby (Chicago: University of Chicago Press, 1991), pp. 457–530; Rafuddin Ahmed, "Redefining Muslim Identity in South Asia," in *Accounting for Fundamentalisms*, ed. Martin E. Marty and R. Scott Appleby (Chicago: University of Chicago Press, 1994), pp. 669–705; T. N. Madan, "From Orthodoxy to Fundamentalism: A Thousand Years of Islam in South Asia," in *Fundamentalisms Comprehended*, ed. Martin E. Marty and R. Scott Appleby (Chicago: University of Chicago Press, 1995), pp. 288–320.

14. Paul R. Brass, *The Politics of India since Independence* (Cambridge: Cambridge University Press, 1990).

15. Paul R. Brass, *Language and Politics in North India* (Cambridge: Cambridge University Press, 1974).

16. T. N. Madan, "Coping with Ethnic Diversity: A South Asian Perspective," in *The Prospects for Plural Societies*, ed. David Maybury-Lewis (Washington, D.C.: American Ethnological Society, 1984), pp. 42–57.

17. Charles F. Keyes, "The Dialectics of Ethnic Change," in *Ethnic Change*, ed. Charles F. Keyes (Seattle: University of Washington Press, 1981), pp. 3–30.

18. The word *Pakistan* was originally an acronym derived from the names of the Muslim majority areas of the northwest, the *K* in it stood for Kashmir.

19. See Raju G. C. Thomas, ed., *Perspectives on Kashmir: The Roots of Conflict in South Asia* (Boulder, Colo.: Westview Press, 1992), and particularly Riaz Punjabi, "Kashmir: The Bruised Identity," pp. 131–52, and Ashutosh Varsheny, "Three Compromised Nationalisms," in Thomas, pp. 3–43, *Perspectives on Kashmir*.

20. Benedict Anderson, *Imagined Communities* (New York: Verso, 1983).

21. Mohammad Ishaq Khan, *Kashmir's Transition to Islam: The Role of Muslim Rishis (1500–1800)* (New Delhi: Manohar, 1994).

22. Seling S. Harrison, *India: The Most Dangerous Decades* (Madras: Oxford University Press, 1960).

23. Clifford Geertz, "The Integrative Revolution: Primordial Sentiments and Civil Politics in the New States," in *Old Societies and New States* (New York: The Free Press, 1963), pp. 139, 141.

24. Harold A. Gould, *Caste Adaptation in Modernizing Indian Society* (Delhi: Chanakya, 1988).

25. A new dimension was added to the story in the early summer of 1995 with the occupation of a major Muslim Sufi shrine in the town of Chrari-Shareef in the Kashmir valley by armed Muslim militants and its subsequently being burned down. The militants, comprising Afghan, Pakistani, and Kashmiri elements, engaged the Indian security forces in armed action. Some were killed and others escaped; and the town, which had been evacuated by the troops, suffered heavy damage. According to Indian government sources, the militants set the fine wooden structure on fire, but the militants denied this. Why would supposedly devout Muslims burn a place of worship? If indeed they did so, the explanation would lie in the contempt in which Islamic fundamentalists hold the saint-adoring and relic-worshipping Kashmiri Muslims, many of whose religious practices derive from the times prior to the conversion of their Hindu ancestors to Islam.

26. See Madan, "The Double-Edged Sword"; "From Orthodoxy to Fundamentalism"; and *Images of the World: Secularism and Fundamentalism in the Religious Traditions of India* (Delhi: Oxford University Press, 1996).

: 4 :

The Rebirth of Religion
and Ethnonationalism in the
Soviet Successor States

Martha Olcott

Problems of nomenclature are frequently an indicator of deeper conceptual difficulties; if we lack even a name for something, then quite likely there is a great deal more about it that we do not understand. Certainly this is the case with whatever has emerged following the dissolution of the USSR in December 1991. Are the fifteen nations that have appeared in its place the shards of a larger unitary nation that broke up, or are these the "captive nations" of an empire that, in dying, disgorged them whole? Are these historical nations that have regained their independence or had it restored to them, or are they some form of lesser ethnic or religious entities, tribes to whom history has briefly handed flags?

Even the most neutral term on which the world initially agreed, the newly independent states (NIS), contains a number of political assumptions and judgments; can any of the Baltic states fairly be described as "newly" independent if the world community had maintained a diplomatic fiction since 1945 that Soviet invasion had put the independence of these states in abeyance but not canceled it? Indeed, virtually all of the "newly independent" nations can point to some period of history, even within this century, that would allow them to argue that they are not newly independent but rather independent once again.

What this nomenclatural difficulty reflects is a deeper problem—that our understanding and evaluation of the processes leading to the demise of the USSR and the consequences following from it depend to a great degree on the vantage point and the political values of the speaker. Religion and ethnicity were highly politicized concepts throughout Soviet history; even to pose the question of how these affected formation of self-identity is to reveal one's assumption that the predominant analyses were incorrect.

Prior to independence, Soviet research on the formation of self-identity sprang from an environment in which "nationality" was listed in line five of every citizen's Soviet internal passport, marking who he or she was just as surely as did lines one through three—family name, given name, and patronymic. At the same time, however, Soviet officials viewed nationalism not only as a political deviation but as something potentially dangerous to the state. At various points in Soviet history, in fact, it was possible even to be jailed, or worse, for advocating nationalism. Endowing ethnicity with political dimensions, as nationalism was understood to do, was viewed as intrinsically damaging to the greater Soviet whole.

The attitude of Soviet scholars and policymakers toward religion was even more hostile, in part because of the official atheism of Soviet ideology. In general, religion as a part of identity was considered to be a vestige of superstition and backwardness and was explicitly rejected as an element of national identity.

At the same time, a small number of Western scholars (the present author among them) saw ethnicity and religion as normal elements of self-identity and attempted to isolate and identify those components of self-identity, particularly among non-Russians, that had political dimensions. Soviet scholars considered these natural categories of self-identity to be pejorative, and they accused Westerners of engaging in "bourgeois falsification."

Intellectual climates began to change in the USSR in the late 1980s, followed by the radical transformation of the political climate. The concept of nationalism, so recently anathematized, has now become the basis of political ideology. To a great degree, however, this acceptance of nationality as a political definer has eclipsed scholarly focus on studies of self-identity just as much as the rejection of it did earlier. Nationality remains a passport category in most of the new states, but even where that form of identity has been formally eliminated, peoples' consciousness of nationalism is, if anything, higher than it was in Soviet times because ethnic membership is now assumed to confer an automatic shared identity. Over the entire territory of the former Soviet Union, in less than a decade, nationalism has gone from being something that people might be ashamed of or afraid to be accused of possessing to being something that people *must* possess lest they be suspected of sedition.

One of the reasons nationality is so charged a category in the Soviet and post-Soviet context is that ethnicity, or national identity, was the fundamental unit of which society consisted. The USSR was composed not of geographical or economic units but rather of republics, each of which bore the name of an ethnic group. For most of Soviet history the authorities maintained the public fiction that these republics were fully sovereign, a fiction with which the world agreed, at least in the case of Ukraine and Belarus, which were seated in the United Nations alongside the USSR. Although this division into smaller, ethnicity-based units was a fiction, the juridical and legislative frameworks necessary to sustain this fiction made it fairly simple for the Soviet Union to divide into new states: boundaries, names, and administrative structures already existed. Moreover, the fact that everyone had a nationality printed on his or her passport made it theoretically simple to determine who was a citizen, at least in the case of the fifteen titular nationalities.

It is sometimes difficult for people of Soviet background to understand the way that ethnicity is recognized only culturally, not legally, in the United States; one is a citizen or one is not, regardless of ethnic origin or self-identity. In the Soviet context, particularly in the years when the USSR was primarily a closed world in which most people never encountered citizens of another state, citizenship was a given scarcely worthy of notice, while nationality was the quality that defined peoples' lives. Indeed, despite periodic official attempts to give adjectival meaning to the word *Soviet*, most ordinary people saw themselves as being Russian, Kazakh, Latvian, or any other of the approximately one hundred national categories on the census forms.

Having created the fiction that it drew its legitimacy from the empowering of its constituent ethnic groups, the Soviet system had to prevent any movement to invest ethnicity with genuine political identity, because of the inevitable danger this would present of a desire for separatism or even a reasonable degree of autonomy. Nationalism presented a definitional political threat to the Soviet system, for which reason any manifestation of national identity that fell outside very narrow permitted confines was branded "deviant nationalism" and punished. Even groups such as the Armenians or the Balts, with a strong ethnic identity and a sense of shared national agenda, had to permit their political agenda to be confined by the realities of Moscow's dictates through most of the Soviet period.

Secession as a Political Tool

As a consequence of the strong Soviet sanctions against it, political nationalism was weak in most parts of the Soviet Union. The only exception was the Baltic states, which had a much more recent experience with independence; indeed, one explanation given for the rise of nationalist movements in Lithuania was the fear of losing the national heritage as the generation that remembered independence was dying out.

While it may have been nationalism, as the term is generally understood, that prompted the Lithuanians to attempt to secede from the USSR in March 1990, it was the failure of the Gorbachev government to force them back in that fed the explosion of nationalist groups and movements. Although this explosion mobilized mass support around nationalist slogans and goals, it thrived on support from the authorities and other elites who saw secessionist movements as a new political tool of enormous utility in the economic struggle raging about the USSR.

The Gorbachev reforms began as a way of increasing the authority of the Communist Party, but by 1990 they had eaten deeply into party credibility. The weakening of central control encouraged a struggle for economic control, particularly as it became clear that the communally held property of this enormous state was going to be privatized and that some form of a market economy was going to be introduced. The emerging ability to control and dispose of economic resources fueled the need to ensure political control of as much territory as possible. It was immediately obvious that in a decentralized system the local elites of independent or autonomous territorial units would be the ones in proper position to control the distribution of wealth. Thus, the local elites had a clear incentive to manipulate the ethnic sensibilities of their particular region and people as one means to gain and solidify territorial control.

That struggle was exacerbated by the composition of the USSR. There were approximately one hundred Soviet nationalities (the list varied slightly from census to census), about half of which had eponymous autonomous territories of one size or another. Most of these autonomous *okrugs*, *oblasts*, and *raions* were within the Russian Federation. The Abkhaz and the Ossets had portions of the Georgian republic, the largely Armenian territory of Nagorno-Karabakh was within the administration of Azerbaijan, and the Karakalpaks had territory in Uzbekistan. Everywhere in the post-Soviet world these smaller "ethnic units" have compounded the problems of state formation and state consolidation.

Of the new states only Russia is a federation, but the nature of its federalism remains poorly defined. Some of the nominal ethnic regions, such as Sakha (former Yakutia), have been content with very nominal sovereignty, while others, such as the Bashkirs and the Volga Tatars, have claimed that their constitution, laws, and dicta take precedence over those of Moscow. One of Russia's federative units, Chechnya, has even asserted the right to secede, although the world has yet to recognize or accept it.

The assertion of national independence in others of the successor states has been even more traumatic; Georgia and Azerbaijan have been nearly destroyed by the efforts of smaller ethnic subunits to achieve independence. In fact, rights of national self-determination need not even be asserted to play a significant political role because of the general conviction across the post-Soviet landscape that to assert the right of secession leads ineluctably to war. The demographics of Kazakhstan, equally split between Russian-speakers and ethnic Kazakhs, make even the subject of federalism threatening to the central authorities, because the notion of empowering the Russian populations of northern Kazakhstan immediately raises the specter of secessionism.

However, the fact that national movements, latent or active, proliferate across the former USSR does not necessarily mean that all of these are movements of national self-determination. Many of the national and ethnic movements of the late Soviet years would likely never have developed had the Soviet Union not been suffering political and economic crises simultaneously.

The Role of Religion

The question of the role played by religious identity in the breakdown of the USSR is more difficult to answer, in part because of the sharp distinctions the Soviet authorities—and the watching world—drew between the growing religiosity of Christians and non-Christians. The Gorbachev-inspired policy of *perestroika* and *glasnost* included a large component of Russian Orthodoxy, if only to combat the growing corruption of public officials. Increased Orthodox spirituality was specifically linked to public honesty and morality, in the hopes that religious discipline might prevail where party discipline had failed.

By contrast, in the case of the non-Russians and most particularly in the case of Islam, state officials saw religion as the cause of corruption and disloyalty, rather than as an antidote. In fact, the Andropov and early Gorbachev years were marked by a strong official campaign against Islam, targeted because the religion seemed part of the wider problems the Moscow leadership was suffering in Central Asia.

Once Moscow put its support solidly behind the revival of Russian Orthodoxy in the buildup to the celebration of the millennium anniversary of Russia's conversion, it was politically impossible not to encourage Islam as well. The faith became accepted as one aspect of the national revival of the various Central Asian, Volga, and Caucasian peoples, but official support was always grudging and somewhat nervous. The Soviet leaders, including those of nominal heritage, were and remain nervous about Islam, partly because they have come to believe Soviet propaganda about the evils of Islam and partly because they took some part in the earlier campaigns against Islam, thus leaving themselves vulnerable to charges of hypocrisy, apostasy, and worse in the changed political climate. Equally important was the official suspicion that Islam as a religion does not easily lend itself to official control, always leaving the faith something of a potential "dark force," at least in the suspicious minds of the rulers.

However, the politicization of ethnic, national, and religious demands was not the cause of the breakdown of the USSR. Rather, the cause was the increasingly obvious ossification or demonstrable unreformability of both the economic system and the political system of the USSR. The economic system had come to the point of paralysis because of the hypercentralization of the state-owned system and because of the irrational linkages, or lack of them, among various parts of the economy. The political system approached a similar paralysis because it was based on an ideology that almost none of the elite believed, even if most of the masses remained adherents. Equally important was the fact that the party authorities were growing increasingly corrupt, which official sponsorship of religious revivals did nothing to stop.

This twin crisis stimulated the increasing politicization of the population along ethnic lines, in a confusing mixture of genuine and provoked nationalism that combined with the growth of a democratic tolerance among a portion of the Russian population to bring down the moribund Soviet system. Even so, save in the Baltics there was no general recognition by the world that the dissolution of the USSR automatically conferred a right of self-determination on the constituent ethnic groups. Independence, after all, is a matter of both declaration and international recognition; the latter for most of the new ex-Soviet states was very slow to come and indeed, in many ways, is still being partially withheld.

This international reluctance to embrace the new states is a reflection of the general geopolitical conviction that new nations are messy and undesirable. They are potentially destabilizing to established economic systems and political systems alike. However much the rhetoric of international diplomacy may say otherwise, the world community values order and predictability far above democracy, especially when changing economic and political systems make democracy volatile and turbulent.

In the mid-1980s it seemed as if the world were entering a period of greater integration, as diplomats and leaders sought new forms of global cooperation on economic, social, environmental, and other issues. Nationalism was widely seen to be something of a relic, a withering survival from an earlier period of competition between neighboring communities that had struggled for control of land and local resources. This was particularly true in the case of the USSR, since virtually no one outside the Soviet Union considered the peoples of the USSR to be true nations. The sole exceptions were the three Baltic states of Estonia, Latvia, and Lithuania, all of which had been independent states from 1918 until 1939. The Western nations had made a show of refusing to recognize the Soviet seizure of these states, permitting the "free" Baltic states a shadow existence of impoverished diplomatic legations, unusable international passports, and periodic assurances of world outrage at Soviet postwar landgrabs. In 1990–1991 the reality of the international community's attitude became clear, however, when no outside states dared to recognize the newly declared independence of Lithuania and then of the other two states.

The world was even less ready to accept national claims from the other Soviet peoples. While there was a general acceptance of the separate ethnicity of at least the European peoples of the USSR, there was no support for the higher claim of nationhood. Ukraine and Belarus had been permitted the fiction of independence for membership in the United Nations and so had some existence. Moldovans had perhaps some world identity, while Georgians and Armenians were known and acknowledged groups. However, the world saw no necessity for these various peoples to become states.

The international community was concerned above all with the democratization of the Soviet Union. There was strong international support for increasing freedom of religion within the USSR and a general consensus in favor of preserving the cultures and languages of the minority peoples. But there was no international support for the political empowerment of the minorities, precisely because that was seen as a threat to Russian attempts to overhaul the USSR. Rising nationalism was also seen to be a threat to the civil rights of Russians living in non-Russian areas, who somehow managed to avoid appearing to be *colonnes*. Another of the strange ironies of the collapse of the USSR is the completeness with which the world seemed to have forgotten that it was the Russians who had invented the communist system and the consequent faith that it placed on the abilities and motivation of Russian democratic reformers to transform or replace that same system. In fact, the general perception of the part played by Russian reformers in the final years of the USSR is somewhat at odds with the reality, because much of the impetus for the human rights and democratic movements originated in the Baltics and was disseminated eastward, sometimes by imitation but frequently because of organizers who had been consciously dispatched to help other nascent organizations.

The widespread enthusiasm with which these organizers were met was a reflection of the aspirations for statehood that most of the peoples within the USSR had been nurturing, despite the difficulties and dangers this had presented, until the last years of Gorbachev. The Ukrainians, the Belarusians, the Armenians, the Georgians, and the Azerbaijanis had sought full independence in the period 1917–1920, when the first Russian empire collapsed. Many had even had states, briefly established though they were, so it was natural for groups in all of them to begin imitating the lead of the Baltics, agitating for independence in 1990–1991.

Indeed, even in Central Asia, which had long been kept one of the most quiescent parts of the Soviet Union, the years 1990–1991 saw an upsurge in interest in national sovereignty. The imposition of Russian control on the region had muddled the history of earlier states in such a way that there were no logical historical "heirs," as there were in Armenia or Ukraine; nevertheless, the Central Asians were aware of the long histories of self-rule of earlier states in the region and were also aware that some peoples, such as the Kazakhs, had also made attempts at self-rule in the period of 1918 to 1920.

Internally, though, the proto-nations of Central Asia were much less developed than were those in the European parts of the USSR. There were at least two major causes for this: the arbitrary boundaries that Stalin had established for these states and the fragility of secular nationalism, which brought as a consequence the strong possibility that Islam might play a large part in revived nationalism. The two problems are aspects of the fact that the pre-Soviet Central Asians had seen themselves primarily as Muslims, whether they were nomadic herders, settled farmers, or city dwellers. Further subdivision tended to be by clan, tribe, and family and thus not national in the way they were in Europe. Identity was not necessarily even linguistically determined, since many Central Asians, particularly in the cities, knew several languages, using Persian and Turkic dialects all but interchangeably.

Stalin's division of Central Asia into five republics had, with time, created some national awareness so that by 1990 most people thought of themselves as Uzbeks, Kazakhs, Tajiks, and so forth. However, there was still no essential tie between those identities and the territory that bore their ethnic name; Uzbekistan in particular has large numbers of its putative nationals living in each of the other Central Asian republics, which immediately raises the destabilizing question of borders.

As disturbing as the possibility of border conflicts may have been, something else worried authorities both in Central Asia and elsewhere—a possible resurgence of Islam. The strongest element of identity to resurface if nationalism were to be stimulated would spring from the region's Muslim past, especially since the region's Muslim clerics had for the most part managed to keep themselves freer of collaboration with the Soviets than had the Orthodox church or other state faiths. This relative autonomy from the state only further increased the attraction of Islam. Indeed, an Islamic Renaissance Party had organized in 1990 and was establishing branches in all the Central Asian states, raising the specter of political challenges against which the ruling elites would have had very little defense.

The international community feared the emergence of political Islam in Central Asia at least as much as did the Central Asian leaders. The withering of monolithic communism as a global security threat had left leaders and military thinkers in search of a replacement; in 1990 and 1991 many had come to the conclusion that Islam would be this enemy. The fear that Central Asia would "go Muslim" further strengthened the preference of the international community to support and strengthen the secularists of Central Asia, most of whom were also the existing party elite. Both within and without Central Asia the greatest concern of the authorities was to define the unavoidable statehood-to-come not in terms of national or religious communities but rather in terms of the existing Soviet administrative boundaries, which had been created to make Central Asia *less* workable, rather than *more*.

There is a discernible distinction in international attitudes toward the relative legitimacy of the claims of the various titular peoples. The Europeans—the Ukrainians, the Belarussians, the Georgians, and the Armenians—gained relatively wide acceptance as true nationalities. The nationalities that gained their present names only in the Soviet period—the Kazakhs, the Kyrgyz, the Uzbeks, and the Tajik—faced much greater skepticism, as did the Azerbaijanis, whose claim to nationhood was never taken as seriously by the international community as was that of the Armenians. Nor was this entirely a product of antipathy toward Central Asia, for Moldova too faced much of the same skepticism.

The case of the Jews was peculiar but also significant. While also not viewed as a nation, they were understood to be a distinct ethnic group, primarily defined by political and religious persecution. Claims based on their ethnic distinction were among the earliest that the international community took up as legitimate, but the concern was never to provide the Jews with a territory, let alone with statehood. Rather the international community attempted by both carrot and stick to achieve guarantees of nondiscriminatory treatment for members of this ethnic group, which would continue to live dispersed throughout society.

As nationalist protests spread through the USSR, the international community responded rather as they had in the case of the Jews, supporting initiatives to secure nondiscriminatory treatment of various ethnic communities, supporting attempts to establish legal bilingualism, and supporting elements of cultural equality, such as provisions for education and civil administration in languages other than Russian. It is very clear, however, that even such solidly established peoples as the Ukrainians, the Georgians, and the Armenians were not seen as having the same right to statehood as had the Poles, Hungarians, Bulgarians, and Rumanians. Even the Czechs, Slovaks, and various Yugoslavs were seen to be natural units for nation-states, despite their mixed ethnicity.

The peoples of the Soviet Union had no basis on which to create such a distinction. Soviet law made no juridical distinction among the various nationalities, so there was no way the state could distinguish between nationalities that had nominal republics, such as the Uzbeks, and those that did not but were demanding territory, such as the Tatars. The Soviet experience had equalized all of its peoples, at least in terms of how they defined their claim to existence: as the tide of nationalism rose, whole groups of peoples could equally stake claim to a given territory. Those claims were buttressed by the *glasnost*-era rewriting of history, conducted on an enormous scale all across the USSR. Particularly after 1991, each of the peoples has set about redefining its history in such a way as to claim as long a historical justification for each state as possible. Thus, the Kazakhs now see their state as a continuation of the rule of the khans of the sixteenth and seventeenth centuries. The Uzbeks have reached even further back, claiming that their ancestors have always been "Uzbeks," rather than simply part of the Turkic tribesmen or Turco-Persian city dwellers who populated Transoxiana.

Economic issues were at least as important as historical ones, however. Even before independence the leaders of the republics had begun to fight for at least partial control of the economic resources on their territory. To gain this control the technocrat-communists of Baltic states began to support the Baltic national revival, for they understood that regional autonomy, even if given for cultural reasons, would have primarily economic dimensions. Although slower to understand the linkage than were their Baltic colleagues, the Central Asian leaders too soon saw that obeisance to Moscow's dictates was costing them any modicum of control of their republican wealth.

In Central Asia the comparatively artificial nature of the Soviet-era nationalities also made the situation somewhat more confusing. In the preindependence period there were strong mass movements in support of cultural revivals, primarily around language issues, and of religious revival, which was seen as a necessary part of national or regional identity. But the nature of ethnic nationalism in the Central Asian context was less certain than it was with the "natural" states, as in the Baltics. The inhabitants of the "natural states"—the Balts and also the Ukrainians, Georgians, and Armenians—viewed themselves as having greater rights to self-rule than did the "contrived" nations, meaning those in Central Asia as well as Moldova.

In response, particularly after 1990, when Lithuania began to press its claim for independence very hard, the Soviet authorities crafted juridical arguments that stressed the legal equality of all the Soviet constituent states, whether "natural" or "contrived." That was the basis of the renewed Union Treaty that Gorbachev attempted to have all the republics sign as a new legal basis for the continued existence of the USSR.

The international community also supported the Soviet attempt to treat all the republics as identical, for the world saw no need to encourage the formation of new states. This was in sharp contrast with the international mood that had prevailed at the end of World War I, when scores of new states had been created from the carcasses of the Austro-Hungarian, Ottoman, and Russian empires, or after World War II, as the British, Belgian, and French empires broke up in Africa and Asia. In fact, as the negative experiences of new nationhood mount in the former Yugoslavia and in the former USSR, the international community comes increasingly to fear demands for national self-determination, casting nervous glances at other large multinational states, such as China and India.

The USSR collapsed far more quickly and completely than anyone would have expected, so almost none of the constituent nationalities had time to prepare for independence. Much as they may have dreamed of statehood in private, most of the ethnic groups in the USSR never believed that they might achieve it, so they never developed a body of "civic fathers" and "founding martyrs" as did the peoples of new states elsewhere. However, once independence came, people were happy to accept it; the collapse of the Soviet Union, if not truly irreversible, would certainly be very dangerous to attempt to reverse. This is true in "contrived" states as well as in the "natural" ones, for independence has been a great equalizer, making the citizens of Turkmenistan as genuinely enthusiastic about their sovereignty as are the Lithuanians.

That is likely to remain the case in the future, even in situations where economic or political crises lead to de facto loss of independence. The economic collapse of states like Belarus, Tajikistan, and Kyrgyzstan has required ceding large amounts of authority to Russia, and even Kazakhstan seeks as much integration with Russia as it can achieve, to stave off the possibility of Russian secession. All these states, though, remain juridically independent and sovereign. For much the same kinds of geopolitical reasons that the world community did not wish to see the new states emerge, they will now not wish the new states to disappear again, especially if they were to be swallowed by force.

The Acceptance of New Nations

The general preference of the world community to see these new nations remain at least as juridical entities is also strengthened by the gradual slackening of nationalism in the new states. None of the new states is monoethnic, and soon after independence each of them faced problems of how to deal with national minorities. The most difficult such group was the former majority, the Russians. No matter how seductive the temptation of cultural retribution may have been, each of the new states soon understood that it could not afford to lose its Russians, who were overwhelmingly the managers, engineers, doctors, teachers, and technicians that the new states needed to survive. Thus, all of the new leaders have had to become advocates of multiculturalism, even in states like Kazakhstan, where federalism, or politically empowered ethnicity, is viewed as a destructive eventuality.

The national minorities also play a role, for issues of cultural autonomy, which were only demands in 1989, by the mid-1990s had become absolute and nonnegotiable. The same is true of religious freedom, which is now taken as an absolute. Certain of the new states, Uzbekistan prominent among them, have redefined the nationalism of the recent past in a way that claims the state has always been more monoethnic than is in fact the case. The Karimov government has made a conscious identification of the present state with earlier states in the same region, thus claiming Uzbekistan as a continuation of the Turkestani emirates of the past, even of the empire of Timur. The Uzbek authorities argue that the expansion of these empires is a model and justification for the strenuous defense of Uzbek national interests both within the present boundaries of Uzbekistan and in Central Asia more broadly.

The other Central Asian states and even more so the international community reject Uzbek imperial ambitions, denying or limiting the right of a national government to defend the rights of their "stranded co-nationals" in other states. This is ironic, for Russia has been extremely successful, both within the Commonwealth of Independent States (CIS) and in the international arena, in establishing a foreign policy based on precisely that right, to defend the interests of ethnic Russians wherever they live. The world's acceptance of Russia's right to interfere in Latvian or Kazakh politics for the sake of the Russians there is based in part on geopolitical realities; not only is Russia far larger and more powerful than is Uzbekistan, but its control of the territories where the 25 million Russians are now "stranded" is quite recent, whereas the Bukharan control of Transoxiana, which the Uzbeks now claim as their precedent for "defending" the Uzbeks of Kyrgyzstan, Tajikistan, or elsewhere, ended between 70 and 125 years ago.

There is another dimension to international support for this Russian policy: the international community perceives Russian nationalism—as opposed to Russian chauvinism—to be secular, tolerant, even pluralistic, and hence the best available vehicle for the democratization of other peoples of the region. Russians furthermore are accorded the rights of great nationhood, which makes their language and history more important than those of the peoples around them or among whom they live. The world generally agrees that others should know Russian language and history, whereas Russians have no corresponding need to know the language and history of others.

As a consequence, the West has ceded to Russia a great deal of authority in the setting of the international agenda for assimilating and incorporating the other new states. Not surprisingly, this has left Russian nationalism and Russian Orthodoxy as the most desirable providers of identity. The other Christian nationalisms, in Armenia, Georgia, or western Ukraine, are viewed more suspiciously, as though they present greater dangers of exclusivity. Even where these nationalisms are largely secular, they still tend to be seen as potentially exclusive in a way that Russian nationalism is not.

The Muslim nationalisms, not surprisingly, are widely seen as the most threatening, inherently nondemocratic and definitionally exclusive form of nationalism. This is particularly true if the nationalism contains a strain of religion, as it does in parts of Turkmenistan and Uzbekistan. The causes for this distrust are many: Western ignorance or prejudice about Islam, condemnation by association with religious exclusivity in other parts of the world, and the fact that in Central Asia the former communist *nomenklatura* are unable to recast themselves as democratic nationalists, as they have done with much greater success elsewhere in the former USSR.

Given the general hostility of the international community to nationalism across the former USSR, especially in Central Asia, it seems reasonable to ask whether the alternative of multinationalism is possible. Given current conditions, the answer would seem to be no, at least if this is to mean truly ethnicity-blind application of policies. However much they may speak of tolerance for other ethnic groups, the public in each of the new states strongly supports the continuation of political domination by the titular ethnic group, now that history has made it a reality. The public and the authorities alike are particularly resistant to appeals to multinationalism that would shift power back to a new minority, which only recently possessed that power as the old majority. Because in the current context multinationalism is usually understood to be a code term for increasing the political power of the local Russians, there is very little official support for what is in fact the handing back of power.

There is also world concern about whether nationalism can be democratic. To date, the question has been framed largely in terms of how to defend the rights of minority ethnic groups against the assertions of power of the new majorities. What is less widely understood is that the question of democracy has not yet been raised on the level of the individual, since membership in one ethnic group is meant to convey a unanimity of attitude. An unresolved question is whether in current conditions it is possible for Uzbeks or Kazakhs to disagree among themselves without violating the integrity of their nationalism.

As has been noted above, the current antidemocratic tendencies of nationalism, enforcing a supposed group of attitudes on all members of a group, are also being manipulated by people in authority, who find nationalism a convenient tool for controlling political and economic access within a given republic. Indeed, the same mechanism is also used within ethnic communities, as clans, families, and regional associates also struggle to maintain and enlarge the spheres of public life that they now control.

The enormous economic and political dimensions of public control color attitudes toward nationalism, both within the former USSR and in the broader international community. In general, forms of nationalism that do not mandate, or even imply, a change in the existing elites are seen as less threatening than those that do. Thus, Yeltsin can be a Russian nationalist and indeed can even be tolerant of more extreme forms of nationalism, because his accession to power is understood to be an expression of that nationalism. Similarly, Kuchma can be a Ukrainian nationalist, since there is nothing in that to contradict his own rule. Even Brazauskas of Lithuania can be a nationalist, while also remaining a socialist, in large part because his form of nationalism, just as is true with Yeltsin and Kuchma, is consonant with use of the local language and advancement of the local history and culture. And most important, it is strongly supportive of the national religious revival.

This last point shows the contrast with Karimov or Nazarbaev. As president of a country that is more than half non-Muslim, Nazarbaev is absolutely unable to embrace the Islamic portion of Kazakh nationalism. And Karimov, whose nation is of nearly 90 percent Muslim origin, cannot become an "Islamist" if only because of his past as a Moscow-appointed enforcer of atheist doctrine. This inability to embrace Islam inevitably leaves the rulers of Central Asia with the conundrum of how to advance only half a nationalism, encouraging language, culture, and history but rejecting or limiting the religion that once formed the core of national identity. Of course, the desire to remove religion from Central Asian nationalism fits neatly into the geopolitical realities of the region, just as it is consonant with the biases of most Western leaders.

After three years of independence for all the former republics of the USSR, it is easy to forget the unique way that independence came about, not as the result of long struggles against a colonial master but rather as the consequence of a collapse of central authority, which in part represented the desire of the dominant nationality was to be rid of the burden of the other peoples. Although nationalism has emerged as a consequence of independence, it is nevertheless possible to ask how strong nationalism really is in the post-Soviet context. In the case of the Baltics it seems that nationalism, as measured by local support for independence at almost any cost, is quite strong. The presence of large nonindigenous populations— up to almost half in Latvia, for example—means that support even there is not universal, so there is a continuing debate on the nature of the state that frequently becomes acrimonious. Are Latvia, Lithuania, and Estonia to be exclusively national states in which everyone speaks the titular language, or are they to be states defined in such a way that the large Russian populations can continue to live as they did in the Soviet period, in all-Russian environments?

For the rest of the former USSR, though, the nature and degree of individual nationalism is much harder to gauge. The former Soviet Union was a stressful, disorienting place in which to live, and the individual republics that have replaced it are little better. People have been subjected to many disillusionments and offered many new truths, all in rapid succession, so it is little wonder that many people have shattered identities. For all that no one believed in it, the identity of "Sovietness" had an elasticity that none of the new nationalisms can provide. Deprived of their former "Sovietness," an enormous number of people have been left without defined identity. The most obvious case is the many people of mixed heritage, who have, for example, Azerbaijani fathers and Armenian mothers or Uzbek fathers and Russian mothers. However, even people of "pure" lineage face grave problems of identity in the new environment: who "is" an opera singer now if he was trained in Moscow but is Kyrgyz? Or a writer, if he wrote in Russian and lives in Moscow but is Azeri? Or an astronaut and career air force pilot if he is Kazakh? The past vice president of Kyrgyzstan was ethnic Kyrgyz but unable to speak Kyrgyz, and the past prime minister of Kazakhstan was Ukrainian, born in Russia, and spoke Kazakh fluently; the conditions of the new nationalism are unable to cope with either.

In the Soviet period, especially in its last days, the nationalism of individual ethnic communities dominated public consciousness. People loudly asserted their rights as Uzbeks or Ukrainians or, indeed, as Russians, equally loudly and contemptuously rejecting the identity of "Soviet man," which the authorities had worked for decades to create. What becomes increasingly clear as the memory of the USSR fades, however, is that for the vast majority of the Soviet population there was in fact a shared identity. There were some small exceptions, mostly among the peoples who had been incorporated into the USSR by force after World War II and then been brutalized into keeping their nationalism invisible, but most people had a sense of shared identity. In the current context it is remarkable how nonethnic that Soviet identity was, even though each people took care to find its "own" hero among the Soviet pantheon—Sverdlov for the Jews, Kunaev for the Kazakhs, and so on.

At the same time, people shared a common environment, knew a common history, and felt a sense of participation in the triumphs of Soviet heros such as Yuri Gagarin, Valeri Brumel, and others. By the end of the USSR most people shared a common language and a common intellectual and political environment. They watched many of the same shows on television, read many of the same books, suffered many of the same tediums and indignities at the hands of similar bureaucrats. Although people did not necessarily share a common culture, elements from various cultures had made solid incursions into the practices of most peoples in the USSR so that, for example, the details of a Victory Day or New Year's celebration, both Soviet additions to most people's calendars, would be broadly familiar to anyone from anywhere within the USSR.

That shared Soviet identity was particularly strong among the elite, many of whom even sacrificed the language and other attributes of their native ethnic identity to gain advancement in the Soviet environment. Many of these people have had to repaint themselves hastily in the current environment, and many more, especially in the arts and sciences, have found themselves painfully stranded between identities. Even at the mass level, where people's primary ethnic identity remained stronger, that Soviet identity of the past is associated with the economic and social security that has now vanished.

This nostalgia for the Soviet identity of the past makes it quite possible for some form of reintegration to succeed, particularly if it were to come about in such a way that formal independence of the new states is preserved. The strongest constituency against reintegration in the present environment is the former "partocrats" who have grown wealthy by trading in the goods, commodities, and resources of which they spontaneously took control. These newly empowered and very wealthy individuals and families are most likely to protect themselves against loss of the economic autonomy they need to continue to thrive by invoking—or indeed by provoking—exclusive nationalism.

The early nationalists, who fought against the communists for the preservation of their languages and cultures, have taken almost no part in this process of enrichment but rather have seen their lives and those of their people grow even worse under the new system. Increasingly, therefore, the real nationalists, embittered by the former partocrats who have used nationalism as a cloak for self-enrichment, are finding common ground with the new communists, who once again are basing their critiques of society on class rather than nationality. Ironic though it may be, the masses of people who in 1989–1991 supported nationalists in order to improve their lives are now turning back to the only segment of the postcollapse political spectrum that is still articulating an internationalist or ethnicity-blind ideology.

The continued economic decline across the post-Soviet territory and the increased differentiation of populations by income may increasingly obviate the one fact that so far has been most remarkable about the resurgence of nationalism across the post-Soviet landscape, namely, that it has been essentially bloodless. As rich and poor grow farther apart, the possibility of social violence will also grow. The willingness of most of the peoples of the former USSR to endure enormous privations is a testament to their deep preference for order above all. This suggests that the post-Soviet populations themselves may decide to seek some form of reintegration if the alternative is to maintain independence at the cost of escalating violence. For most of the peoples of the USSR, the history of the development of nationalism is so recent that it is difficult to gauge the price at which the various peoples value their independence. The shared experience of a pan-national Soviet past, which in retrospect provided prosperity and security, may translate into a very low social threshold at which people will prefer reintegration, even domination, to the questionable virtues of independence.

: 5 :

Religion and Nationalism in the Balkans: A Deadly Combination?

Gabriel Partos

In the early 1990s a large part of the then disintegrating federation of Yugoslavia became engulfed in a terrifying fratricidal war. Since then the flames of that war have consumed thousands of lives in Croatia and Bosnia-Hercegovina,[1] put to the torch scores of villages, and reduced to rubble entire cities. Millions of people have been forced from their homes, fleeing the fires of military combat, expulsions, and atrocities in the first full-scale fighting to erupt in Europe since the end of World War II. It took over four years of armed conflict before the Dayton peace accords of November 1995 brought an end to this devastating round of fighting and held out hopes for a long-term settlement.

The land thus ravaged for the third time in eighty years has for centuries been a meeting place for—or a faultline between—a bewildering array of different nations, ethnic groups, languages, cultures, and religions. Occupying an area roughly the size of Oregon or Britain, the former Yugoslav federation was home to six republics; eighteen sizable national and ethnic groups (not counting those that declared themselves Yugoslavs) with almost the same number of separate languages among them; and three major religions—Roman Catholic Christianity, Orthodox Christianity, and Islam—in addition to small Protestant and Jewish communities.

Although these three faiths have for centuries competed or coexisted with each other in the Balkans, religion has been one of the least discussed components of the wars of the Yugoslav succession that broke out in 1991. This is understandable. The federal Yugoslavia that Marshal Josip Broz Tito created at the end of World War II and that collapsed forty-six years later was a state ruled by a communist establishment. Its Marxist-Leninist ideology was militantly antireligious, and it had produced a largely secular society, particularly among the growing ranks of city dwellers. Few would attribute the demise of communist rule and the disintegration of the federal state either to religious conflict or to demands for greater freedom of conscience. This dramatic transformation was largely the outcome of conflicting national aspirations and mutual fears among different ethnic groups that returned to haunt the Yugoslav peoples against a background of steady economic decline. The emerging nationalist leaderships of the republics stirred up and then exploited these aspirations and fears in the struggle for power and territorial gain. No leader has done so with greater determination or ruthlessness than Serbian president Slobodan Milosevic.

Yet the role of religion and the religious communities cannot be ignored. Religion has been and remains a key component of national identification in the Balkans. For that reason it cannot be separated, as though under laboratory conditions, from nationalism. So what role has religion —and the religious—played in the Yugoslav drama? To what extent has religion contributed to reawakening the rival brands of nationalism from their slumbers? In what ways have religious figures tried to bring about reconciliation and peace? Since most of the adversaries would identify themselves with different faiths, can the conflicts in the former Yugoslavia be described as religious wars? And what impact has the fighting had on religion in the area?

Some of these questions will be addressed in this chapter. The discussion will focus on the three ethnoreligious groups that have played the roles of the protagonists in the bloody tragedy that has unfolded in the former Yugoslavia: the Christian Orthodox Serbs, the Roman Catholic Croats, and the Muslim Slavs of Bosnia. Because of space limitations the other national and religious communities must act as extras, with "walk-on" parts only, in this focused and selective telling of the drama; thus, the Catholic Slovenes and Hungarians, the Orthodox Slav Macedonians and Montenegrins, and the mainly Muslim Albanians will appear only in passing. Similarly minimized in this essay are the religious and national complexities of the rest of the Balkans, as seen in their domestic and cross-border interaction in Romania, Bulgaria, Albania, and Greece.

Three national communities—the Serbs, the Croats, and the Muslim Slavs—have been at the heart of the latest conflict in the former Yugoslavia; they are linked by the closest of ties. All three belong to the southern Slav family of people, have lived as neighbors or intermingled for centuries, and speak different variants of the same language. During the Yugoslav era that language was commonly known as Serbo-Croat (or to assuage Croatian sentiments, as Croato-Serbian); now it is once again referred to as Serbian or Croatian and, increasingly, in the case of Bosnian Muslims, as Bosnian.

What divided these national communities is their divergent histories and traditions and their separate religions. Among those who profess religious beliefs or affiliations in this region, it is difficult to envisage a Serb who is not Orthodox, or a Croat who is not a Catholic. As for the Slav Muslims of the former Yugoslavia, they are unique among Muslims in the world in having their very identity as a separate nation tied directly to the religious and cultural traditions of Islam. That remains the case even though in recent years there has been a tendency to revert to a geopolitical rather than a religious form of identification—Bosniaks. In all three cases religion has been one of the driving forces in building up a sense of ethnic identity. Today it remains a powerful symbol of national distinctiveness even among the large numbers of nonbelievers who continue to accept the broad cultural traditions of their more pious ancestors' religious beliefs.

The Historical Background

The Serbs and Orthodoxy

Through much of Serbian history—through triumph and defeat—the Serbian Orthodox Church, which acquired *autocephalous*, or independent, status in 1219, played a key role in creating, sustaining, or resurrecting the various forms of Serbian national identity.[2] In the Middle Ages the very existence of a separate Serbian Church underlined the power of the Serbian empire. During nearly five centuries of Ottoman Turkish occupation that followed Serbia's defeat at the battle of Kosovo in 1389, the church remained the only institution that was perceived by many Serbs as looking after their interests. On several occasions it acted as a rallying point for revolts against Turkish rule. Following the crushing of one of these uprisings in the late seventeenth century, it was Patriarch Arsenije of Pec who led the large-scale migration of Serbs from Turkish-occupied Kosovo to areas under the control of the Austrian Habsburgs.

As Serbia gradually regained its full independence from Ottoman rule in the nineteenth century, the Orthodox Church lost its preeminence as the representative of the national cause. Instead, it became in some ways an auxiliary of the new Serbian state. But it continued to help rally support to the cause of Serbian unity, seeking as its ideal a common state for Serbs living not only in Serbia itself but also in the neighboring lands still belonging to the Ottoman or Habsburg empire.

As these age-old empires collapsed at the end of World War I, the dreams of those who had advocated the unity of the southern Slav peoples finally came true. The kingdom of Serbs, Croats, and Slovenes emerged in 1918 and was rebaptized Yugoslavia—the land of the southern Slavs—

eleven years later. The ideal of southern Slav unity that embraced the Orthodox Serbs as well as the Catholic Croats and Slovenes and the Muslim Slavs had no particular attraction for the more exclusivist Serbian Orthodox Church. The authorities' attempt to create a supranational Yugoslav identity had little in common with the Orthodox Church's long-standing goal of gathering all Serbs under one protective umbrella, where they would be masters of their own fate and free to foster their Orthodox religious and cultural traditions. On the other hand, interwar Yugoslavia did have something to commend itself to the Orthodox Church: it brought the Serbs together in one state largely dominated by Serbs. Yugoslavia had a Serbian dynasty, Serbian politicians took the lion's share in key government posts, the army was led by Serbian officers, and the bureaucracy was dominated by Serbian officials.

In the 1930s relations between the government and the Orthodox Church were clouded by Yugoslavia's plans to conclude a concordat with the Vatican. The Orthodox Church opposed the accord. It was concerned that the concordat would give the Catholic Church equal standing with the Orthodox Church within Yugoslavia and that the Catholic hierarchy would then be able to exploit its advantages — a more sophisticated organization, a better educated clergy, and more extensive international contacts — to make inroads among the Orthodox believers. Working hand-in-hand with the Serbian opposition parties, the Orthodox hierarchy managed to scupper the concordat in 1937.

The Orthodox Church feared Catholic proselytism among its faithful. What happened within years of the attempted concordat surpassed even its worst nightmares, however: Hitler's invasion of Yugoslavia in April 1941 destroyed the country. From the rubble there emerged a nominally independent Croatia led by a fascist regime, under German tutelage, which viewed Serbs as enemy number one. About one-quarter of all Serbs now lived under Croatian rule in a state that also included Bosnia. Croatia's fascist authorities, known as the Ustashe, embarked on a campaign to eliminate the Serbs as a nation from their territory through mass expulsions, conversions to Catholicism, and killings.

The Orthodox Church took a tremendous battering in the cycle of violence unleashed by this policy. Since Serbian nationhood was under attack, its symbols and leading proponents quickly became the main targets of the anti-Serbian campaign. Though some of the Orthodox clergy were themselves involved in encouraging anti-Croat or anti-Muslim atrocities, on the whole they were far more often victims than perpetrators of crimes. The Ustashe murdered scores of Orthodox priests and destroyed hundreds of churches. As a result of frequent references to the traumatic events of those years, the legacy of that war has continued to haunt the Orthodox clergy and their flocks to this day. But side by side with its enormous losses, the Orthodox Church emerged from the war with enhanced prestige among many Serbs because it had shared their sufferings in full.

The Croats and Catholicism

The close association between the Catholic Church and Croatian nationalism has a somewhat shorter history. Under the Ottoman empire the Serbs surrendered their independence to the Muslim Turks; as religion was a crucial distinguishing factor between ruler and the ruled, the Orthodox Church formed a natural vanguard to represent Serbdom. Most Croats, meanwhile, came under the rule of fellow Catholics, first Hungarian and then the Austrian Habsburgs. For this reason religion was not a natural focus for Croatian national sentiments, except in Bosnia where they lived under Muslim Turkish rule. Besides, in many ways Catholicism was and still is a universalist religion, with a leader in the Vatican who was not supposed to be tied to any particular nation.

The rise of nationalism in Eastern Europe in the nineteenth century made a profound impression on Croatia's political landscape, however, and the revival of interest in national literature and history resulted in a more important role for the church. Through the pulpit and the press, many of the Catholic clergy were among the most active participants in the educational process that accompanied the awakening of nationalism. They were also in the forefront of resisting the Magyarization campaign of Croatia's Hungarian rulers in the last decades of the century. (During the same period the Slovene clergy worked in a similar way to counteract their Austrian rulers' Germanization drive.)

Yet this national awakening in Croatia was not initially exclusivist. Leading figures in the Croatian renaissance, such as Josip Juraj Strossmayer, bishop of Djakovo, sought an alliance with the neighboring southern Slav peoples. Their ideal was a Yugoslav union that would integrate the nations that spoke the same language or related languages. Though he was a leading cleric of the Catholic Church, Strossmayer adopted an ecumenical approach, stressing what Catholic Croats had in common with Orthodox Serbs instead of dwelling on their differences.

Strossmayer's commitment to what was to become the Yugoslav ideal was influential among Croatian (and Slovenian) intellectuals. Gradually, however, a brand of specifically Croatian nationalism gained the upper hand within the Catholic Church. In the chaotic conditions that followed the collapse of the Austro-Hungarian monarchy in 1918, however, the Croats as well as the Slovenes threw in their lot with Serbia. Yet the newly established Serb-dominated southern Slav state failed to satisfy the aspirations of most Croats, and the Catholic Church in Croatia soon began to share its people's growing disappointment. For many Catholics the failure of the Yugoslav state to conclude a concordat with the Vatican was symptomatic of the Orthodox Church's dominant position.

The Croatian Catholic hierarchy therefore welcomed the declaration of Croatian independence that accompanied Nazi Germany's defeat of Yugoslavia in April 1941. Alojzije Stepinac, archbishop of Zagreb, was among those who threw caution to the winds and gave a spiritual blessing to Croatia's new pro-German authorities, the Ustashe. But the reign of terror the Ustashe unleashed against Serbs, Jews, Gypsies, and their political opponents came as a shock to Stepinac and the rest of the hierarchy. Stepinac protested to the authorities against these atrocities but to little avail. The Catholic hierarchy also condemned the Ustashe's practice of mass forcible conversions of Orthodox Serbs to Catholicism. The protests were muted, however, and the Catholic hierarchy's commitment to Croatian independence remained firm—regardless of the price. Moreover, there were numerous sympathizers with the Ustashe in the ranks of the younger clergy, some of whom fought alongside the militias and took part in forcible conversions and atrocities. Perhaps the greatest failing of Stepinac and the hierarchy was their inability or unwillingness to discipline these wholehearted supporters of Ustashe crimes. The Catholic Church's ambivalent attitude helped weaken its position at the end of the war.

The Muslim Slavs

For the Muslim Slavs of the former Yugoslavia the linkage between religious belief and ethnic identity has been a relatively recent development. The large majority of Muslims are the descendants of people converted to Islam following the Turkish conquest of Bosnia-Hercegovina in the fifteenth century. In that region the process of conversion was facilitated by the absence of a strong monolithic religious tradition. Catholicism, Orthodoxy, and the local Bosnian Church—largely Catholic in its traditions though independent of Rome and often accused of the Bogomil heresy—vied with each other for adherents, creating a tolerant climate in which religious beliefs were relatively weak. Nor was there a stable system of religious institutions or a hierarchy to fight a rearguard action against the onward march of Islam. (The success of the Franciscans in keeping Catholicism alive in Hercegovina followed the collapse of the Catholic diocesan hierarchy in the region.)

Having adopted the faith of their conquerors, the Muslim Slavs had little in the way of a separate ethnoreligious tradition to look back to in order to rally them against the Ottoman Empire when the ideology of nationalism began to gain ground in the nineteenth century. In any case, they were among the main beneficiaries of that rule. Unlike their Christian Slav neighbors, they had the opportunity to take government posts. Bosnia's landowners, merchants, and professionals were predominantly Muslims. Indeed, on the occasions when they rebelled against their masters in Istanbul, it was usually to safeguard their long-standing privileges in the face of modernizing tendencies that were being adopted by the Ottoman rulers. While many Orthodox Serbs were beginning to dream of independence as part of a greater Serbia and the Catholic Croats were showing interest in a union with Croatia or with a broader group of southern Slav nations, the Bosnian Muslims remained largely unmoved by these national projects.

The withdrawal of the Turks from Bosnia-Hercegovina and their replacement by Austro-Hungarian rule in 1878 gave the first jolt to Muslim self-awareness. The Bosnian Muslims feared they would lose their privileged position as their protectors departed the region. In fact, their new rulers were keen to cultivate the Muslims' loyalty, but Vienna also did its utmost to cut them off from Istanbul by creating the post of *reis-ul-ulema* to head the Islamic community in Bosnia. Meanwhile, the Muslims came under increasing pressure from both Serbs and Croats who wanted to adopt them as their own—as fellow nationals whose ancestors had converted to Islam but who remained essentially Serbs or Croats, though of a different faith. To protect their national identity from this pressure (including several conversion campaigns by Catholics) and to safeguard their trading and land-holding privileges, the Muslims formed a National Muslim Organization. It gave loyal support to the Habsburgs and tended to cooperate with the Croats, while the Serbs gravitated increasingly toward Belgrade.

Although the Muslims were proud of their separate religious identity, this rarely extended to having a separate ethnic consciousness before the interwar period. By then growing pressure from Serbs and Croats was giving the Muslims an increasing sense of their own ethnonational identity. During World War II, Bosnia-Hercegovina was incorporated into Croatia. The Muslims, now regarded as Croats of the Muslim faith, tended to fight with the Croats against the Serbs. But others formed their own local self-defense units or joined Tito's multiethnic communist partisans who were waging war against the German and Italian occupiers and against the Ustashe and the Chetniks, armed groups of Serbian nationalists whose atrocities sometimes rivaled those of the Ustashe. In the eyes of the partisans and the Serbs, the Islamic religious community was not as closely associated with Croatia's fascist authorities as was the Catholic Church.

The Communist Era

The Serbs

The end of the war inaugurated a speedy transition to communist rule in Yugoslavia. President Tito's objective was to weaken the power and influence of the religious communities, to undermine their association with ethnic particularism, and to reduce their role in society. Education was considered the key battlefield in the fight for people's hearts and minds. Starting in 1945, the state began to take control of church schools and abolished religious instruction therein.

The authorities had a relatively easy task in reaching an accommodation with the Serbian Orthodox Church. Although the church's standing among Serbs received a major boost during World War II because it bore witness to their own sufferings, the loss of many priests and church buildings meant that the Orthodox hierarchy had to concentrate its efforts on rebuilding its pastoral work. In any case, the Orthodox Church had a long tradition of working in hostile conditions. Rendering unto Caesar what was Caesar's—an Orthodox tradition—meant that it made little difference whether the ruler was a Muslim emperor or a communist president. Moreover, the Orthodox Church's regionalism—its independence from an international hierarchical structure—made it easier for the authorities to portray it as a patriotic institution that could coexist with the communist regime.

Under the long-serving Patriarch German, the Serbian Orthodox Church returned to its quietist traditions. It avoided posing any direct challenge to the authorities. The hierarchy's acquiescence in communist rule was one of the reasons behind the split in the ranks of the Orthodox Church that occurred in 1963, when the Serbian émigrés' diocese, based in the United States and Canada, declared its autonomy from the mother church. That schism was not healed until nearly three decades later when the heads of the two churches jointly celebrated divine liturgy in Belgrade's Saborna cathedral in 1992. The celebrations were a national as much as a religious occasion; generations of Serb soldiers, from veterans of World War I to the Serb militias who only a few weeks earlier had fought in Croatia, were represented in strength to celebrate the renewed unity of Serbian Orthodoxy.[3]

Yet for reasons more to do with nationalism than religion, during the communist era the Orthodox Church had remained a thorn in Tito's side. In the postwar period the Yugoslav authorities were busy creating a federal state, based on checks and balances between the different national and ethnic groups, so as to lay to rest the memories of the prewar "First Yugoslavia" that was dominated by the Serbs. The six republics created after the war as constituent parts of the new federation included Macedonia, which before the war had belonged to Serbia. As part of the process of nation-building, Macedonians, with the support of the federal authorities, began to agitate increasingly for their own Orthodox Church. The Serbian Orthodox Church resisted that pressure on national and organizational grounds. It continued to regard Macedonians as southern Serbs—it still does so today—and its leaders could not countenance a second schism following the rupture of relations with the Serbian émigré hierarchy. So it refused to recognize the creation of the autocephalous Macedonian Orthodox Church, which broke away from its Serbian parent organization in 1967.

Curiously for a communist leadership, the Yugoslav federal authorities (and even more so the Macedonian government) gave vigorous support to the establishment of the Macedonian Orthodox Church, whose first head, Metropolitan Dositej, received a decoration from President Tito. It was a robust demonstration of how an atheist regime would, for reasons of interethnic balance, promote the interests of a religious institution.

The Muslims

Another group that benefited from the authorities' support was the Muslim community. Once again the reason for bolstering the Muslims' sense of identity had much to do with the tactics of cutting down to size the more powerful national groups—the Serbs and the Croats. It was to undermine these two communities' encroachments on the Muslims' separate identity and to prevent the revival of their potentially dangerous rivalry in Bosnia that the Yugoslav authorities promoted the Muslims to a position of equal status with the other, long-established nations. After decades of uncertain or changing ethnonational affiliation, Muslims were, for the first time, allowed to register as "Muslims in an ethnic sense" in the 1961 census. Seven years later they acquired the status of a nation. Thus, they joined the Serbs, Croats, Slovenes, Macedonians, and Montenegrins as one of the constituent peoples of federal Yugoslavia.

This level of identification between religious and ethnic affiliations, unique in Islam, was the result of political expediency. As with the Macedonians, once again it was the communist state, atheist and internationalist in its ideology, that gave its blessing to the creation of a new nation and reinforced its links with religion. Unlike the case of the Macedonians, in which a religious institution followed in the wake of establishing a national identity, in Bosnia the Muslim religion served as the basis for the shaping of a new nation. True, the communist authorities did their best to belittle the role of religion, emphasizing that it was only part of a much broader Muslim tradition with its own culture and customs, many of whose adherents had no religious beliefs.

Like the Serbian Orthodox Church, the Islamic religious community caused little trouble for Tito's leadership. As the extent of the regime's support of the Muslims expanded from the 1960s onward, the Muslim community's loyalty to the authorities also increased. Not only did the Muslims' status improve, but they also gained increasingly better access to Muslim countries around the world. In exchange, the communist authorities exploited their Islamic establishment's contacts with Muslim countries for diplomatic and commercial gain. During the four decades after the end of World War II more mosques were built in Yugoslavia than either Catholic or Orthodox churches, even though Muslims were, as they still are, considerably outnumbered by the adherents of both Christian churches.

The Croats

In contrast to the Orthodox Serbs and the Muslims, the Catholic Church, particularly in Croatia, acted as an energetic opponent of the communist regime in Yugoslavia. Although its ambivalent attitude to Ustashe rule seriously weakened its standing among Croats at the end of World War II, the communist authorities soon came, unintentionally, to its rescue. Of mixed Croat-Slovene parentage, Tito was fully aware of the Catholic Church's strengths through its links with the Vatican, its well-educated clergy, and its tradition of involvement at all levels of society. Tito wanted the Catholic Church in Yugoslavia to renounce its loyalty to the Holy See and become an independent body. When Archbishop Stepinac refused, he was put on trial in 1946 on charges of collaboration with the Ustashe leadership and was sentenced to sixteen years of hard labor.

In the eyes of most Croatian Catholics the trial turned Archbishop Stepinac into a martyr and the Catholic Church into a symbol of the struggle for Croatian nationhood. That trend accelerated after the crushing in 1971 of the "Croatian Spring," a movement that combined demands for greater national autonomy with political liberalization. With the political leaders of that movement purged and the main cultural organization behind it banned, the Catholic Church remained the sole institutional standard-bearer promoting a more vigorous adherence to Croatian national traditions. The rise of the controversial Medjugorje cult in Hercegovina, where apparitions of the Virgin Mary have been reported since 1980, was symptomatic at the time of the intertwining of emboldened Croatian nationalism, religiosity, and anti-communism.

The Religious Communities and the Disintegration of Yugoslavia

The Catholic Church and Nationalism

As the steady decline of the Yugoslav communist system began to gather momentum after Tito's death in 1980, the Catholic Church was relatively well placed in Croatia to step into the new ideological vacuum through its fidelity to a system of values that set it apart from the country's rulers and through its close association with Croatian national traditions.[4] In contrast to the Serbian Orthodox Church, it had adjusted comparatively well to the new, more secular society by its involvement in education, youth groups, and social activities. When the communist authorities began to tolerate organized political opposition to their rule in 1989, the Catholic Church quickly made its preferences known, albeit often in an oblique way. Although in the run-up to the first free elections in the spring of 1990 the Catholic commission Iustitia et Pax instructed the clergy not to take an active part in politics,[5] many priests gave at least veiled support for the noncommunist parties. Gestures and ceremonies frequently counted for more than words. The election of the anticommunist and nationalist Franjo Tudjman as president of Croatia was celebrated in May 1990 at a solemn mass in Zagreb's cathedral; Croatia's new leader sat in the front pew as Cardinal Franjo Kuharic bestowed his blessing on the new administration, and the cardinal later sat next to the president at a festive session of parliament to inaugurate the new president.[6]

The Catholic Church's support for President Tudjman's administration was fully reciprocated. Within weeks of his inauguration, President Tudjman publicly acknowledged its role as the only institution in society to have resisted communist rule and to have kept alive Croatian national consciousness. A year after taking office, the new government set in motion the introduction of religious education in all primary and secondary schools, starting in the 1991–1992 school year.[7]

Croatia's war of independence from Yugoslavia cemented the alliance between the new nationalist administration and the Catholic Church and reinforced the bonds between church and people. Zelimir Puljic, bishop of Dubrovnik, summed up this close identification at the time the Yugoslav army was besieging his city, the "Pearl of the Adriatic," by noting: "The history of the Croatian people has been Catholic history. And to fight for Croatia is to fight for Catholicism."[8] A number of priests went further in their rhetoric, portraying the war as part of an age-old struggle between Western civilization and Eastern barbarity, thereby ignoring the rich heritage of linguistic and cultural ties between the two nations that were not at war. One Zagreb priest's definition of what the war was about reveals much about popular attitudes: "Here is where the West ends and the East begins. We in Croatia are fighting to stop the East from invading the West."[9] Another Catholic clergyman from Zagreb gave the conflict an even clearer religious significance: "This war is a conflict between two worlds, between Croatia as defender of Western and Catholic culture, against the world of Orthodox *Vyzentia* [Byzantium], which is a renegade thing."[10] By magnifying the differences between the Catholic and Orthodox traditions, many priests made reconciliation between the warring sides a great deal more difficult.

A number of Catholic clergymen were to voice far more inflammatory remarks during the war in Bosnia that pitted Croats against Muslims. Animosity was particularly strong among some Franciscans (though this attitude was not shared by the Franciscan hierarchy). Father Zovko, for example, the Franciscan protector of the Medjugorje visionaries, had served eighteen months in prison under the communists. In an open letter to the International Court of Justice he wrote of the Muslims: "They are conducting a horrible Muslim *mujahideen*, a diabolical *jihad* program to destroy everything that is Croatian and Catholic."[11] Another Franciscan at Medjugorje described the conflict to a group of pilgrims from England as "a war of the baptized against the unbaptized; of Christ against the anti-Christ."[12] Similar remarks, reminiscent of the medieval crusaders' frame of mind, were uttered not infrequently in former Yugoslavia the end of the twentieth century.

The Catholic Church and Reconciliation

In the period leading up to Croatia's independence the Catholic Church did much to bolster the national cause. During the war itself it helped preserve morale among the Croats by providing justification for the fighting on grounds of self-defense. It also gave solace to the victims of the conflict. Though the Croatian Church hierarchy refrained from identifying the aggressors with the Serbs, it did little to further reconciliation. It was during the three-cornered fight in Bosnia, when Croat nationalists adopted a more aggressive stance, aimed at annexing parts of Bosnia, that the Catholic Church espoused a more unambiguously antiwar policy. Working in tandem with the Vatican, the Catholic Church leadership in Croatia denounced attempts to carve up Bosnia between Croatia and Serbia. Cardinal Kuharic denounced the fighting between Muslims and Croats as being "totally without justification" and reiterated his support for the internationally recognized state of Bosnia.[13]

In Bosnia itself, Archbishop Vinko Puljic of Sarajevo, spiritual leader of the republic's Catholics, resisted the steady pressure from Croatian nationalists to abandon his flock in the besieged Bosnian capital and move to the Croat-ruled area in the southwest of the republic, which would have given the church's blessing for the Croat nationalists' self-proclaimed ministate of Herceg-Bosnia. Even the Franciscans of Bosnia, who kept Catholicism alive during more than four centuries of Muslim Turkish rule and later helped sustain the traditions of Croatian nationalism in the region, dismissed the temptation to line up behind the Croatian extremists. The superiors of the Bosnia-Hercegovina Franciscan province remained firm in their adherence to Bosnia's territorial integrity in their opposition to "all secret or secretly forged and proposed plans" for the division of the republic and in their resistance to forced population transfers on ethnic grounds.[14]

Besides its opposition to Croatia's expansionist plans in Bosnia and its repugnance of a further round of bloodletting, the Catholic Church's denunciation of the Croatian nationalists in Bosnia was driven by its realization that the project was ultimately self-defeating. In a contest with the mainly Muslim Bosnian government army it appeared very likely that the Croat nationalists would be able to secure only their heartland in Hercegovina. But two-thirds of Bosnia's Catholic Croats had traditionally lived elsewhere, in smaller and more scattered communities in central and northern Bosnia. They were bound to suffer huge losses (as they did in the course of fighting with the Muslims in 1993) and were in danger of being sacrificed as a result of allowing the minority of Croats in their Hercegovina stronghold to have their own state.[15]

The Catholic Church also showed a greater degree of detachment from the Croatian state authorities when fighting in Croatia resumed in 1995. Although the church hierarchy did not question Croatia's right to retake by force the areas of the country that were under Serbian control, Cardinal Kuharic did, somewhat belatedly, condemn the atrocities that had been committed against Serbian civilians during and after the recapture of the Krajina region in August. In remarks pointedly addressed to a congregation of Croatian army officers and soldiers he said that nothing could justify harming defenseless human beings, whatever their ethnic origins.[16]

The Serbian Orthodox Church and Nationalism

Although the wars in Yugoslavia in the first half of the 1990s pitted Orthodox Serbs against Catholic Croats and Bosnian Muslims, the first blood in the current round of conflict was shed within Serbia itself; the victims were the mainly Muslim ethnic Albanians of the formerly autonomous Kosovo province. Scores of Albanians, who outnumber Serbs in the province nine to one, were killed by Serbian security forces when they protested against the abolition of their autonomy in 1989–1990. The revival of Serbian nationalism began in the wake of agitation by the Serbian Orthodox Church that Kosovo, which it had long regarded as the heartland of Serbian civilization and which was home to its most ancient monasteries, was being taken over by ethnic Albanians. Members of the Serbian Orthodox hierarchy accused the Albanians, predominantly Muslims but with a minority of Catholics among them, of pursuing a religious campaign against the Serbs. They compiled lists of attacks on Serbian Church property and clergy as part of their struggle to protect Serbian interests in Kosovo. In the process they tended to exaggerate the scale and gravity of such incidents.

From the mid-1980s onward the Orthodox Church's warnings were echoed by influential Serbian intellectuals, and they were eventually adopted by Slobodan Milosevic, the Serbian leader. By the time the six-hundredth anniversary of the medieval Serbian monarchy's defeat by the Ottoman Turks at the battle of Kosovo was commemorated in June 1889, Serbia's communist president stood shoulder to shoulder with Orthodox prelates to demonstrate to the world the unity of revived Serbian nationalism. Almost a year later, when President Milosevic received a delegation from the Orthodox Synod to discuss ways of overcoming the uneasy legacy of church-state relations from the communist era, the clerics expressed the hope that the Serbian government's new tougher policy toward the ethnic Albanians would provide a solution to the problems experienced by Serbs and the Serbian Orthodox Church in Kosovo.[17]

The Serbian Orthodox Church also adopted an active role as the Serbo-Croat conflict gradually unfolded in 1990. It raised its voice against President Tudjman's Croatian nationalist administration, which was elected to office in the spring of 1990. Serbian Church dignitaries objected to the new Croatian constitution, which curbed the cultural and educational rights of that republic's Serbian community. Although several of the Serbian Church's objections to the new Croatian government's policies were justified, the negative way in which the Orthodox hierarchy went about expressing its disapproval only poured oil on the fire. It refused to recognize the democratically elected Croatian authorities and boycotted ceremonial occasions that not only the newly favored Catholic hierarchy but also its Muslim, Protestant, and Jewish counterparts attended.[18] As in Kosovo in earlier years, its claim of assaults on the clergy and property of the Serbian Orthodox Church and on Serbs in general were out of all proportion to the true scale of incidents of that kind.

At a time when there was a desperate need for calm and tolerance to prevent and later to halt the new round of fighting between Croats and

Serbs, the Serbian Orthodox Church did much to whip up latent interethnic fears and prejudices. Its pronouncements frequently recalled the horrors of Ustashe crimes during World War II; indeed, before the outbreak of war in 1991, some of the Serbian Orthodox clergy compared, without any justification, the fresh wave of minor harrassment against ethnic Serbs in Croatia with the Ustashe atrocities inflicted on them nearly five decades earlier. The Serbian Orthodox Church also concentrated on the uniqueness of the Serbs' suffering through history, comparing their fate with that of the Jews. It constantly took the Catholic Church to task for its failure to apologize for what the Serbs regarded as its pro-Ustashe conduct during World War II.[19] At a time when the Serbian forces, better armed and on the offensive, were committing far greater crimes than were their Croatian counterparts, Patriarch Pavle justified their revolt against Croatian rule as though they were under imminent threat of extermination. "The victims of genocide and their former, and perhaps future, murderers can no longer live together," he wrote in a letter to Lord Carrington, then chairman of the international conference on Yugoslavia.[20]

Such was the devotion of the Serbian Orthodox Church to the cause of nationalism that it even broke with President Milosevic when the Serbian leader began to adopt more flexible policies on the issue of uniting Serbian lands. The rift started with the acceptance by the Belgrade leadership in January 1992 of the UN-brokered cease-fire in Croatia. The accord left more than one-quarter of Croatia under Serbian control, and the regions within this self-proclaimed republic of Serbian Krajina were designated UN-protected areas. For President Milosevic the deal provided for the continuation of effective Serbian rule in Krajina with the demarcation lines policed by the UN, and it left him with the option of trying to annex these regions into a greater Serbia or yielding them up to Croatia as part of a future bargain with his Croatian counterpart, Franjo Tudjman.

The Orthodox hierarchy took the side of militant Serbian nationalists who denounced Serbia's president for selling out fellow Serbs in Croatia.[21] (In fact, from the perspective of radical Serbian nationalism, their fears turned out to be well founded. Three years later, in 1995, Croatia recaptured most of its Serb-controlled areas, and in doing so it faced virtually no opposition from Slobodan Milosevic.) The Orthodox Church had meanwhile continued to insist on the unity of Serbdom, which would be built on a joint state of all Serbs living in Serbia, Croatia, and Bosnia. It could not accept the Belgrade leadership's more sophisticated diplomacy and half-measures. Few members of the Orthodox hierarchy went as far as Bishop Atanasije, who denounced President Milosevic as "a traitor and an impertinent man," adding, "the sooner he leaves, the better for Serbia." The bishop derided Milosevic and his defense minister for having "suddenly become pacifists" and accused them of having "betrayed Krajina and Bosnia."[22]

Although the violent language of Bishop Atanasije's attack on President Milosevic was not, on the whole, shared by the rest of the Serbian Orthodox hierarchy, the spirit of his stand was fully adopted by most of them. The three-year-old "unholy alliance" between the communist-turned-nationalist Serbian president and the Holy Synod of Bishops came to an end when the latter turned openly against Milosevic and demanded his resignation.[23] In June 1992, Patriarch Pavle, along with scores of Serbian Orthodox nuns, joined thousands of opposition demonstrators in Belgrade who were demanding the government's replacement.

Thereafter it came as no surprise that the Serbian Orthodox Church should have adopted a more inflexible approach to the prosecution of the war against the Muslims in Bosnia than had the skillful tactician, Slobodan Milosevic. During the multiparty elections of 1990—well before the conflict began—a group of Serbian Orthodox bishops from Bosnia had urged their followers to vote for candidates who would promote the national and religious aspirations of Serbs in the republic.[24]

That meant support for the Serbian Democratic Party, the political organization that was later to spearhead the breakup of Bosnia by its refusal to recognize the Bosnian people's vote for independence in the referendum of February–March 1992. The Serbian Orthodox Church continued to play a prominent political role after the outbreak of war in Bosnia. Several clerics attended the meetings of the Bosnian Serbs' assembly, which rejected two separate international peace plans—the first in May 1993 and the second in July 1994. When President Milosevic moved, half-heartedly in 1993 and with greater determination in 1994, to cut off supplies to his recalcitrant and increasingly independent-minded protégés in Bosnia to persuade them to accept two different international peace plans, the Serbian Orthodox Church denounced him for endangering the unity of the Serbian people. In a clear gesture of solidarity with the diehard Bosnian Serb leadership, the synod held a meeting in Banja Luka, one of its strongholds, in November 1994 shortly after Serbia had cut off aid to them.[25]

The Orthodox hierarchy returned to the attack against President Milosevic in the wake of the Croatian Serbs' defeat at the hands of the Croatian army in August 1995. A statement issued by the synod denounced the "vile, neo-communist" government in Belgrade for "doing nothing to save its people."[26] And in the case of Bosnia, the Orthodox leadership remained close to the local hard-line Serbian political establishment, sharing its fierce opposition to many aspects of the Dayton peace accords—so much so that shortly after the peace agreement was signed, the synod revoked Patriarch Pavle's earlier endorsement of President Milosevic as the representative all Serbs, within and outside Serbia, in negotiations with the international community.

The Serbian Orthodox Church and Reconciliation

Like the Catholic Church, the Serbian Orthodox Church made numerous declarations in favor of peace and reconciliation. However, practical examples of interchurch cooperation were relatively few and far between, partly because the Orthodox feared that the Catholic desire for ecumenical progress concealed a missionary purpose. Moreover, the Orthodox hierarchy's calls for peace tended to be qualified by its insistence that any settlement should be just and fair. But the Serbian Orthodox Church's definition of a just peace involved the unification of all Serbian lands: the creation of a greater Serbia from Serbia itself, Montenegro, and the Serb-inhabited areas of Croatia and Bosnia. Such an objective, involving the annexation of large parts of these two former Yugoslav republics into Serbia, was considered unjust by the Croats and Bosnian Muslims. It was also viewed as a threat by other countries in the region that feared Serbian expansionism and by international powers that were concerned for the stability of the Balkans.

The appeals for peace issued by the Serbian Orthodox Church remained highly ambiguous. Shortly after the war in Bosnia broke out, Patriarch Pavle told his congregation in Belgrade that "the Serbian Church had never taught its people to grab other people's property but to fight for what is sacred to them."[27] Yet the Orthodox dignitaries had made it clear on numerous occasions that they considered the war in Bosnia "sacred." A year later the patriarch admitted in his Easter message that in the Bosnian war there were "crimes and criminals on all three sides." The remark understated the Bosnian Serb nationalists' paramount responsibility for most of the atrocities; in the same statement the patriarch denounced the international community's support for the territorial integrity of Croatia and Bosnia "as obstacles to a peaceful and just solution to the conflicts in these territories." The patriarch also justified the Bosnian Serbs' aggression, their ethnic cleansing of mainly Muslim-inhabited areas, with the rhetorical question "How can someone who is defending his ancestral home be an aggressor?"[28]

Close links between state and church were also reflected in the coincidence of improved relations between Serbs and Croats. In early 1994 there was a limited rapprochement between rump-Yugoslavia and Croatia when the two states set up interest-representation sections in each other's capitals. Almost at the same time, Metropolitan Jovan, head of the Serbian Orthodox Church for Croatia and Slovenia, who had fled Zagreb during the fighting of 1991, returned to the Croatian capital on what he described as "a mission of peace." His service was attended by Croatian parliamentary officials and a representative of the Catholic Church.[29]

The end of fighting in Bosnia provided another fresh opportunity to begin to restore links among the various religious communities, with the aim of contributing to the country's spiritual reconstruction. Within a month of the peace treaty signing, Metropolitan Nikolaj, Bosnia's senior Orthodox prelate, crossed into the government-held part of Sarajevo to officiate at the Orthodox Christmas celebrations in January 1996. It was his first visit across the confrontation lines since his appointment four years earlier, during which period he had frequently bestowed his blessing on the Bosnian Serb troops. Meanwhile, his long absence had disappointed many Serbs loyal to the Bosnian government side, who felt they had been abandoned by their spiritual leaders.

Metropolitan Nikolaj praised Sarajevo's tradition of harmonious interethnic relations, but in the immediate aftermath of his sermon the Serbian Orthodox Church gave few signs that it wished to live up to this ideal. On the contrary, as five districts of Sarajevo were transferred from Bosnian Serb control to the Muslim-Croat federation and the vast majority of local Serbs left the area, in part because of their hard-line nationalist leaders' scorched earth policy, the Orthodox parish priests made no attempt to stem the exodus. The priests locked their churches and left with their congregations, some promising to return one day with an Orthodox army.[30]

The Islamic Community

The loosening of restrictions on political activities that accompanied the collapse of communism in Yugoslavia released the pent-up social energies of the two major Christian churches. The Serbian Orthodox Church returned to a more active advocacy of Serbian national rights, often at the expense of Yugoslavia's other nations. The Catholic Church in Croatia became closely identified with Croatia's struggle for independence and in the process often proved insensitive to the aspirations of the local Serbian community.

The Islamic community had no such urgent national political objectives.[31] After all, it represented all the ethnically diverse Muslims of Yugoslavia. Ethnically, it was divided between the two largest groups, the Muslim Slavs and the Albanians, as well as smaller communities, including Turks and Gypsies. But for two million Albanians, including a minority of Catholics, the conflict with the Serbs was fundamentally a national matter involving the territory of Kosovo, where most of them have traditionally lived. The more than two million Muslim Slavs, the vast majority of whom lived in Bosnia and in the neighboring Sandjak region of Serbia and Montenegro, had no strong national aspirations that would upset the delicate balance of Yugoslavia's interethnic relations. On the contrary, the Muslim Slavs were among the main beneficiaries of Tito's federal system. They had been promoted to the status of a nation, they enjoyed a considerable share of power in Bosnia, and their traditionally poverty-stricken republic had received a large share of the funds distributed from the federal budget. However, the Muslims' ascendancy in Bosnia did have a negative impact by provoking concern among the other national communities.

The Bosnian Muslims had little to revolt against in the federal Yugoslavia and much to lose by its disintegration. It was the departure of Slovenia and Croatia from the federation in 1991 and the prospect of living in a Serb-dominated rump-Yugoslavia that propelled the Bosnian Muslims' drive for independence.

The majority of Muslims regarded their Islamic identity as more of a cultural than a religious matter. Even among the devout, religious belief and practice were considered to belong to the realm of the individual's conscience, not something to be dictated by the authorities. True, the Islamic revival of the 1980s in the Middle East and elsewhere had generated among Bosnian Muslims (and Muslims elsewhere in Yugoslavia) a greater sense of belonging to a specifically Islamic community. A mosque-building program, financed by countries such as Libya and Iran, had contributed to this process.

Although Islamic fundamentalism and extremism made few inroads into Bosnia, there was a movement among Muslim intellectuals who wanted Bosnia to be declared a Muslim republic in the way that each of the other five republics was closely linked in ethnic identity, religion, and even in its official name to the largest ethnonational group among its population. Bosnia remained the exception, principally because it was the only republic without a national community that formed an overall majority among its inhabitants. (The 1991 census listed Bosnia's ethnic composition as 44 percent Muslim, 31 percent Serb, and 17 percent Croat.) The most notable event in the communist authorities' struggle against Muslim nationalism had been the trial in 1983 of thirteen Muslim intellectuals who had supported the views expressed in *The Islamic Declaration*, written by a Sarajevo lawyer, Alija Izetbegovic. The tract urged Muslims to return to Islam and called for the establishment of an Islamic order, though one in which non-Muslim minorities would "enjoy religious freedom and every protection" and "only in countries where the Muslims represent a majority of the population."[32]

As president of Bosnia after 1990, Alija Izetbegovic gave no indication that he had any intention of trying to implement *The Islamic Declaration*, though his opponents accused him of harboring such plans. He could hardly have done so, as he was initially governing in coalition with the national parties of Bosnia's Serbs and Croats. Even after the main Serbian party left his administration, ethnic Serb representatives remained part of his multiethnic government, as did Croats during a period in 1993 when Croatian nationalists turned their backs on the central government in Sarajevo. Through war and peace, President Izetbegovic has been doing his utmost to project the image of a leader who is committed to the survival of a multiethnic and multireligious state. At the same time he has been trying to match this effort with a commitment to strengthen his fellow Muslims' religious and national identity. This has proved on occasion a difficult balancing act, but overall, given Bosnia's continuing ethnic diversity, the identification of the Islamic religious community with the Bosnian republic has remained far more tenuous than the links between the Christian churches and the state in Croatia and to a lesser extent in Serbia.

Moreover, the Muslims of Bosnia, along with their fellow religionists in Albania, have remained stubbornly opposed to any displays of fundamentalism, extremism, or even, in most cases, strict adherence to the religious and quasi-religious tenets of Islam. Those who are not secular in outlook tend to be followers of the Hanafi school of orthodox Islam, the most tolerant wing within the Muslim world. Drinking wine of *rakija*, the popular local brandy, is as widespread as smoking among the vast majority of Muslims. Women long ago discarded the veil, and apart from some of the rural population, they wear makeup and Western clothes. Many nominal Muslims attend Christian church services.[33] "Islam is different here than it is anywhere else: it's Europeanized," said Franjo Komarica, the Catholic bishop of Banja Luka, where Muslims and Catholics have both been the victims of ethnic cleansing by the Serbs. "Our Muslims are very far from fundamentalism."[34]

The Muslim religious community, furthermore, has never had the clear hierarchical structure of the Christian churches and has taken less of a lead on matters of politics than the Catholic and Orthodox dignitaries. In general, the Muslim religious leadership in Bosnia has remained steadfast in its backing for President Izetbegovic, supporting a war that it regarded as a just, defensive struggle against Serbian aggression. Criticism has been muted, with the exception of some clergy from outside Bosnia. Hamdija Jusufspahic, the Belgrade-based spiritual leader of Serbia's Muslims, criticized the mainly Muslim political leadership in Sarajevo for breaking away from Yugoslavia, saying that "it was clear that independence would lead to war and great suffering."[35]

The International Religious Background

The Vatican

The Holy See has played an active and at times controversial part in the events that surrounded the disintegration of Yugoslavia and the outbreak of fighting. Initially, it showed a great deal of enthusiasm for Slovenia's and Croatia's drives for independence. Within a week of Croatia's referendum in favor of independence in May 1991, Pope John Paul II received President Tudjman in a private audience at a time when the war clouds were already gathering on the horizon.[36] Thereafter, during the six-month war in Croatia that followed the Slovenian and Croatian proclamations of independence at the end of June 1991, the Vatican made it clear that it was in favor of granting them diplomatic recognition. It did so in an unexpected move on 13 January 1992, two days before the European Community member-states assembled to grant their long-expected recognition. Thus, the Vatican became one of the first states to acknowledge the two mainly Catholic countries' claim to independence.

The Vatican's backing for the independence of Slovenia and Croatia was motivated by its support for the principle of national self-determination. The peoples of both republics had voted overwhelmingly for independence. There was also a strong belief that international recognition for Croatia would help bring the war to an end because it would transform the Yugoslav military on its territory from a security force trying to rein in a secessionist republic into a foreign occupation army. Indeed, the run-up to the deadline for international recognition of Croatia in early January 1992 coincided with a cease-fire agreement in the republic that included the withdrawal from Croatia of all Yugoslav troops.

But the Holy See's policy was also guided by its affinity for two predominantly Catholic republics. Croatia, in particular, had prided itself on being a bulwark of Christianity and had been awarded the title *antemurale Christianitatis*, the rampart of Christendom, by the medieval papacy. Both countries had emerged from two generations of communist rule and were now led by politicians, some of whom had close links with the Catholic Church. Yet three months later, in April 1992, the Vatican gave an example of its impartiality by being among the first states to extend recognition to Bosnia, a country where Catholics formed a minority. Apart from support for the principle of self-determination, with nearly two-thirds of Bosnia-Hercegovina's population voting for independence, early recognition was motivated by the hope that such a move might help to prevent the outbreak of war. That hope was not to be fulfilled.

Seen from the perspective of Belgrade, the Vatican's approach to the Yugoslav crisis took on a sinister character. The Serbian media had been accusing the papacy of waging a conspiracy, together with Germany and Austria, to dismember Yugoslavia and undermine the Serbian Orthodox Church. Even though the Vatican was at pains to point out that its decision to recognize Croatia and Slovenia was not directed against Yugoslavia, the reaction from Belgrade was hostile. The government described the recognition as "direct interference in the internal affairs of Yugoslavia."[37]

The Vatican again provoked controversy a few months after the outbreak of the war in Bosnia, when Cardinal Angelo Sodano, its secretary of state, made remarks that implied the Holy See's support for outside military intervention to stop the atrocities. He declared that "the UN and the European nations have the duty and the right to intervene to disarm those who want to kill . . . to hold back the arm of the aggressor."[38] Cardinal Sodano's apparent backing for the use of force in Bosnia was followed within days by several denials from the Vatican that it was in favor of military intervention, but the incident reinforced the Serbs' widespread perception that the Holy See remained implacably hostile to them. That feeling was reawakened when the pope himself returned to the theme of foreign intervention in early 1994 in the wake of a tragic incident that resulted in the deaths of six children in Sarajevo. He called on the international community to do "everything humanly possible to disarm the aggressor." (Later still, the same message was repeated with even greater vigor after the fall of the virtually defenseless Muslim enclave of Srebrenica to the Bosnian Serbs in July 1995, when the pope declared that those who failed to act against acts of barbarity risked falling into "the acts of ignominy.")[39]

Such statements increased distrust toward the Vatican in the ranks of the Serbian Orthodox Church. Hostility, mixed with suspicions about the aims of the papacy, accounted for Patriarch Pavle's opposition to Pope John Paul's planned visit to Belgrade in September 1994, which was to be part of a three-nation tour of Serbia, Bosnia, and Croatia with the purpose of preaching reconciliation among the Orthodox, the Muslims, and the Catholics. But Patriarch Pavle vetoed the visit to Serbia on the grounds of the Vatican's alleged responsibility for the breakup of Yugoslavia, the papacy's implied call for punishing Serbs, and the Catholic Church's failure to apologize unambiguously for its involvement with the Ustashe during World War II.[40]

The pope's hoped-for visit to "the martyred city," as he called Sarajevo, was called off at the last minute for an additional reason: the Bosnian Serbs' leaders failed to provide the required security guarantees. Apart from sharing Patriarch Pavle's concerns, they had no intention of allowing the pope to focus the world's attention once again on the sufferings of a city that their forces had been besieging for two-and-a-half years.

The projected tour of Belgrade, Sarajevo, and Zagreb might have pro-led John Paul II with a steady platform of support from which to pro-im his ecumenical message of peace. With only Zagreb left on his itinerary, he was out on a limb. Although in his sermons the pope chose to dwell on what he called "the thousands of unbreakable ties" between the peoples of the region and condemned nationalist intolerance, his pastoral trip to staunchly Catholic Croatia elicited opposing political interpretations from the Croatian and Serbian authorities and media.[41] Even before John Paul's arrival, President Tudjman said the pope's visit signified his support for Croatia's independence and for its struggle to restore its sovereignty over areas under Serbian control.[42] Although the pope's utterances had no such pro-Croatian slant, for most of the huge crowd of faithful who attended the mass he celebrated in Zagreb there was no doubt that this was a papal endorsement of their national struggle.

Meanwhile, the Serbs, whose Orthodox Church representatives declined to attend the mass, also chose to ignore the pope's message of reconciliation and interpreted his visit in line with their long-held views. Their disapproval extended to the pope's praise for the late Cardinal Alojzije Stepinac, a prayer at whose tomb in Zagreb cathedral was part of John Paul's itinerary.

The Orthodox International

The Serbian Orthodox Church has continued to view the Vatican as an adversary bent on spreading Catholicism with renewed fervor following the collapse of communism, and this could be opposed only by rallying the Orthodox peoples. Patriarch Pavle sought to enlist help on a visit to Russia in 1994, when he suggested that a mission of Russian journalists and observers be sent to the former Yugoslav republics to present the international community with what he considered objective information, on the grounds that the Western media often treated the Serbs unfairly.

Though the overall expectations of the Serbian Church hierarchy for help from fellow Orthodox nations may not have been entirely fulfilled, the backing that the Serbian cause has received in the 1990s has come primarily from traditionally Orthodox countries, such as Greece and, to a lesser extent, Russia. The Russian Orthodox Church has repeatedly demonstrated its moral support for the Serbs, including the occasion of Croatia's campaign in 1995 to recapture its Serb-held areas.[43] This has been part of a broader expression of sympathy and backing that has gone well beyond the confines of the Orthodox Church. And for the most part, this support has reflected political, not religious, considerations. Greece's long-standing friendship with Serbia has been reinforced by its fears about Turkey's emergence as a regional military and economic power. Athens has been engaged in building up a counterweight to a Turkey that has been increasing its influence not only in countries with large Muslim popula- tions—Albania and Bosnia—but also in other parts of the Balkans. Greek support for Serbia and for the Bosnian Serbs has taken many forms, from political declarations to mediation efforts that included hosting a confer- ence in May 1993 that came close to clinching Bosnian Serb acceptance of the Vance-Owen peace plan.

Russia's backing for Serbia has been motivated less by the perception of common interests and long-standing links that have influenced Greece. Moscow's policy has been guided by a desire to see Russia recognized as a world power in the post-Soviet era. For that reason it could not afford to leave the Balkans in the Western sphere of influence. By pursuing a pro- Serbian policy, such as advocating the lifting of UN sanctions on Belgrade long before the Dayton peace accords were signed, the Kremlin wanted to emphasize that it was not following a Western and increasingly American orientation.

Russia's backing for Serbia, often on little more than the rhetorical level, has also been motivated by domestic policy considerations. Politi- cians would vie with each other to appeal to the nationalist constituency by recalling the ties that bind Orthodox peoples together. Oleg Soskovets, Russia's first deputy prime minister at the time, assured Patriarch Pavle during the Serbian Church dignitary's visit to Moscow that "the Russians and the Serbs are brothers . . . and have the same confession."[44]

Yet the "Orthodox International" has not been united either on the political or the religious level, partly because of different interests and partly because of the absence of a spiritual unifying force outside the inde- pendent national churches. The Former Yugoslav Republic of Macedonia (FYROM) has been one of the clearest cases of discord between countries in which the majority of the population have Orthodox affiliations. The Serbian Orthodox Church has never recognized the Macedonian Ortho- dox Church's secession from it in 1967. By denying that the "obstinate schismatics" of the Macedonian Orthodox Church represent an autocepha- lous religious community, the Serbian Orthodox Church has continued to question the Slav Macedonians' separate national identity.

Meanwhile, the Belgrade authorities kept up the pressure on Skopje by their refusal until the spring of 1996 to recognize FYROM. This was partly out of solidarity with Greece, which had for long opposed Macedonia's choice of name, fearing that it harbored a claim to its northern province of the same name. Another reason was to test what concessions might be gained from Skopje in terms of the Yugoslav succession issue—the share-out of the previous federation's assets.

Because of these differences there has been no support for the Serbian cause from the Macedonian Orthodox Church, with which the Serbian Orthodox Church broke off all relations in July 1995, nor from FYROM, which adopted a largely neutral stance in the Bosnian and Croatian conflicts. Nor have other traditionally mainly Orthodox countries, such as Romania and Bulgaria, shown much sympathy for the Serbs. They have been anxious to establish their Western credentials in the run-up to negotiations on joining the European Union (EU). They have had little interest in emphasizing the cultural and historical differences that would be seen as possible obstacles on the way to integration with the West—a problem Greece, already an EU member, has not had to worry about.

The Muslim World

There have also been differences among the Muslim countries' attitudes toward Bosnia behind the facade of unity in support of fellow Muslims in the Balkan state. Bosnia is the farthest outpost of Islam in Europe; it lies north and west of two other traditionally Muslim countries, Turkey and Albania. Unlike either of those two countries it has been led since 1990 by a prominent Muslim thinker, Alija Izetbegovic, who had clearly set out his views on how an Islamic state should be organized twenty years before he gained power.

However, Izetbegovic had written about enforcing Islamic law and values in countries where the majority of the people were Muslims, which was not the case in Bosnia. During the war, Izetbegovic was trying to hold together a Muslim-led but multiethnic coalition in Sarajevo. That arrangement has become more complicated since the establishment of the Bosnian Muslim–Croat federation in March 1994 and then in the wake of the Dayton accords, which envisaged a central government that would be composed of the Muslim-Croat federation and the Bosnian Serb republic.

Whatever the intricacies of the government in Sarajevo, in the course of the war most Muslim countries saw it as representing primarily fellow Muslims who were the main victims of ethnic cleansing and religious persecution. Muslim countries and Islamic nongovernmental organizations provided humanitarian aid for Bosnia, helping to sustain the government side through the most difficult days of the war.

Besides economic aid, some Muslim countries were also involved in sanctions busting during the UN's wartime arms embargo to help redress the huge imbalance in stocks of weapons that favored the Bosnian Serbs.

Iran was one of the main suppliers of weapons to Bosnia; Turkey and others were also involved in sanctions busting.

Overall, though, the volume of arms supplies from Muslim countries to the Bosnian government army remained limited; particularly in the area of heavy weapons the disparity in the balance of forces continued largely unchanged throughout the war. Several members of the Organization of the Islamic Conference repeatedly threatened to flout the UN arms embargo, but in the end they never did so publicly. Meanwhile, a few Muslim countries with strongly anti-Western policies—first and foremost, Libya and Iraq—remained conspicuously neutral, and Baghdad may well have been involved in oil and arms deals with Belgrade.

The Muslim countries' involvement in helping the Bosnian government remained more limited than Sarajevo would have liked because many had more urgent problems to deal with at home or in their immediate neighborhood than in distant Bosnia. For others the Bosnians' non-Islamic, European way of life was a disincentive for making a big effort to provide assistance.

Even after the war ended, there was little initial response from Muslim countries, apart from Turkey, when the United States, at a conference in Ankara in March 1996, tried to line up financial assistance to equip and train the Bosnian federation army. Yet the Muslim factor has been an important element in the international context of the Bosnian crisis. Washington's support for the Bosnian government has been motivated to some extent by its desire to undermine Muslim criticism of the West: that it was allowing aggression and atrocities in Europe only because most of the victims happened to be Muslims.

During and after the war, America was also eager to enlist Muslim countries, such as Bangladesh, Malaysia, Pakistan, and Turkey, to provide peacekeeping troops, either for the UN Protection Force (UNPROFOR) or since the Dayton accords, for the multinational peace implementation force (IFOR). The purpose of this was to allow moderate or pro-Western Muslim countries a chance to help Bosnia and to give them a stake in a settlement while keeping out Iran, which had repeatedly offered to send troops.

The presence of small numbers of Iranian and other foreign Muslim fighters was another important issue for Washington, which remained concerned that anti-American elements among them might pose a threat to IFOR's U.S. contingent. It was only after a six-month delay, in June 1996, that the U.S. administration finally certified that all foreign Muslim fighters had left Bosnia, thus removing the last obstacle to the supply of U.S. economic aid for Bosnia's reconstruction.

The Impact of War

The wars in Croatia and Bosnia have had a devastating effect on the peoples of the two republics. By the time fighting was brought to an end with the Dayton peace agreement at the end of 1995, the conflagration in Croatia had cost well over fifteen thousand lives; estimates for that in Bosnia ranged from fifty thousand to more than two hundred thousand. Over three million people, of a combined population of nine million, had become refugees—the largest population movement in Europe since the end of World War II.

The destruction wrought on places of worship has also been catastrophic. The statistics may not be entirely reliable because fighting or continued occupation have made access to many areas difficult, in some cases even after the Dayton peace accords. Besides, the figures for the devastation and deaths come from the political authorities representing the religious communities that suffered them, and these claims may in some cases be exaggerated. But the magnitude of the devastation is not in doubt.

According to official Bosnian statistics, 1,115 mosques and other buildings of a Muslim religious character were destroyed or damaged during the war; the corresponding figures for the Catholic and Serbian Orthodox churches were 309 and 36, respectively. Official statistics in Croatia for the period before the recapture of the Serb-held areas in 1995 refer to 232 Catholic churches and other buildings having been destroyed or damaged; the corresponding figure for the Serbian Orthodox Church was given as 20. Following the 1995 campaigns, the Croatian press reported that in the areas retaken from Serb control 161 Catholic churches and other buildings had been destroyed or damaged as against 15 Orthodox buildings. In contrast to these figures, during the war, Serbian Orthodox Church officials reported losses at 435 buildings in Croatia and Bosnia, though these figures were not borne out by subsequent findings following the recapture of large Serb-held areas by Croatian and Bosnian government troops in the two republics in 1995. The Bosnian Muslims also claimed that 50 of their imams had been killed and dozens put in detention camps by 1994.[45]

Although some of the places of worship were destroyed in the course of fighting, many others were deliberately razed to the ground to sweep away all vestiges of the religion with which the defeated national group was closely linked. Destruction of this kind was part of a campaign to prevent the return of refugees who had been forced to flee by the process of ethnic cleansing. Buildings with a religious purpose provide a focus for communal life for the faithful and a link with their national culture for nonbelievers. Once their mosques or churches are destroyed, refugees are less likely to want to go back to their hometowns.

However, not all sides adopted this form of warfare with the same determination. During and after the recapture of Croatia's Krajina region by the Croatian army in 1995 many Serbs' homes were put the torch, but only a handful of Orthodox churches were damaged. By contrast, virtually all Catholic churches had been destroyed in the region during the years of Serbian rule. Like ethnic cleansing, the war against the buildings of the other religious communities was pursued with the greatest ferocity by the Serbian side. In the Bosnian town of Banja Luka, the Serb nationalists blew up all sixteen of the local mosques. Meanwhile, work began to build an Orthodox cathedral to replace the one razed during World War II by the Germans and the Ustashe.[46]

The Religious Revival

The killing and imprisonment of clerics and the physical destruction of places of worship were not the only effects the war had on the religious communities. It also contributed to a religious revival which had already received a boost before the conflict erupted with the dissolution of the communist federal state and its replacement by mostly nationalist regimes in the individual republics. These new administrations were eager to bolster their popular support by cultivating good relations with the religious hierarchies. President Tudjman's conservative government in Croatia was well placed ideologically to exploit its affinity to the Catholic Church. Nor did President Milosevic, a lifelong communist functionary, appear to find it embarrassing to flirt with the Serbian Orthodox Church when that suited his purposes. President Izetbegovic, author of the controversial *Islamic Declaration*, for which he had been imprisoned during the communist era, had acquired the best possible Muslim credentials even before his ascent to power, and this helped him forge close links with the Muslim clergy when he gained office.

The religious hierarchies responded positively to the nationalist governments seeking the clergy's support for their policies, particularly when these administrations had a conservative agenda to establish a clear break with the communist era. That was the case, first and foremost, in Croatia, less so in Bosnia and least of all in Serbia. (But while relations between the authorities and the Serbian Orthodox Church deteriorated in Serbia after 1992, ties between the ultranationalist Bosnian Serb leadership and the same church remained very cordial.) To varying degrees in the different republics, the religious establishments all benefited from greater access to the media; they regained at least a foothold in education; acquired a say in legislation on social issues, such as abortion; and built up political influence. But as the fighting dragged on, the religious leaderships found their various degrees of identification with the aims of political authorities an increasing source of embarrassment. The Catholic Church took issue with the Croatian government's undeclared policy of helping its protégés in Bosnia carve up that republic along ethnic lines. Cardinal Kuharic vigorously condemned the fighting between Bosnian Croat nationalists and the mainly Muslim forces in 1993; pressure from the Catholic Church contributed to President Tudjman's volte-face in early 1994 in reviving the Muslim-Croat alliance.

The Serbian Orthodox Church had already denounced President Milosevic in 1992 for giving insufficient support to the militant Serbs in Croatia and later also in Bosnia. A few years earlier the Orthodox dignitaries had considered Slobodan Milosevic, a born-again nationalist, the only guarantee for protecting the interests of all Serbs. By now they felt that a number of other Serbian politicians had given proof not only of their commitment to the nationalist cause but also of their ability to lead viable political parties.

The close links between state and religious hierarchy in all three cases (especially in the early phase of the conflict) were only one reason for the religious revival. The war itself polarized people; the everyday experience of fighting, siege, and atrocities made most members of the various ethnic groups emphasize their national and religious differences. For others, however, faith has provided solace to help them cope with the personal tragedies war dispensed on such a massive scale.

It is not possible to quantify the extent of the religious revival because no reliable statistics are available on this topic. Communist Yugoslavia stopped recording its citizens' religious affiliations after the census of 1953. Research carried out later was handicapped either by the small size or the regional limitations of the sample. One survey in the mid-1980s found that two-thirds of the respondents nominally belonged to a religious community, although among those who thus identified themselves the proportion of believers ranged from 62 percent for those from Catholic families to 44 percent of those from Muslim families and only 26 percent of those from Orthodox families.[47] Other surveys, though producing different results for the proportion of believers, confirm the relative strengths of religious belief, with Serbs the least likely to be religious and Croats the most.

Churches and mosques during the war were filled with far more worshippers than before the outbreak of fighting. At the height of the Yugoslav army's siege of Dubrovnik, the city's Catholic bishop, Zelimir Puljic, noted: "The people are coming back to the Church. They are more afraid and more religious."[48] Courses in Catholic religious education attracted thousands of adults. Some were eager to catch up with knowledge that was denied them during the communist era, others were, no doubt, hoping that it would be to their advantage in the newly conservative and nationalist Croatia to be seen as being good, practicing Catholics.[49]

Among Muslims there has also been a greater interest in prayer and attendance at the mosques. The huge number of funerals caused by the disproportionately high level of war dead among the Muslims also brought many otherwise nonpracticing Muslims closer to their faith. Irfan Ljubijankic, the Bosnian foreign minister at the time, declared to a receptive audience in Tehran that "the return of Bosnians to Islam was the only positive point about the war" in his country.[50] But as in Croatia, where the profession of Catholicism became an informal prerequisite for promotion to a whole range of public service posts, a display of Islamic religious observance could also gain a whole range of benefits for Muslims who might otherwise show no interest in religion. This became more important as President Izetbegovic's Muslim Party of Democratic Action consolidated its grip on appointments to positions of authority in the areas controlled by the Bosnian government side. So if religion has been flourishing since the beginning of the war, especially in Croatia and Bosnia, this was at least in part for secular reasons.

However, a campaign spearheaded by foreign Islamic volunteer fighters (*mujahidin*) and charity workers to instill the virtues of Muslim fundamentalism among Bosnia's highly Europeanized Muslims has turned out to be largely a failure. Even in the Muslim strongholds of Travnik and Zenica it has had only limited success. During the worst period of fighting between Croats and Muslims in this area in 1993, many of the local Muslims accepted stricter forms of observance; some women put on the veil, and they sent their children to Koranic classes. They did so under pressure from the *mujahidin*, who were fighting for them, or to receive food aid from the Islamic relief agencies. When the Muslim-Croat war came to a halt in early 1994 and the need for foreign help was no longer so desperate, most of the local Muslims reverted to their much more relaxed, prewar form of Islam.[51]

The majority of the Bosnian Muslim clergy have shown no sympathy for the fundamentalist project. At a time when some Muslim intellectuals suggested that polygamy might be the answer to the decline in the Muslim population caused by the war, Mustafa Ceric, the head of Bosnia's Islamic religious community, dismissed the idea with the words: "Polygamy has never been part of our culture."[52] But the greater political and social influence of the Muslim clergy has contributed to attempts to tighten up on the Bosnian Muslims' traditional laxity of observance. Since 1994 there has been a noticeable trend toward banning the sale of pork, criticism of mixed marriages between Muslims and Christians, and attacks on "European trash" such as alcohol and prostitution.[53] The inflow of large numbers of conservative Muslim refugees from the countryside into the traditionally multiethnic, cosmopolitan, and tolerant cities provided a relatively receptive audience for attempts of this kind to impose a more stringent form of Islamic observance.

Conclusions, Prospects, Dangers

The fighting in Croatia and Bosnia has been accompanied by a veritable war of words between adversaries who have set out to prove whether the conflict in the Balkans is religious or not. In general, those who claim the bloodshed is rooted in a clash of faiths accuse the other side of waging a crusade or a jihad to repress or exterminate people with different beliefs. Even before war broke out in Bosnia, Haris Silajdzic, the republic's foreign minister at the time, rebutted allegations from Serbs who claimed that Muslims were bent on establishing an Islamic state. Silajdzic declared: "our only *jihad* is one for a democratic, secular state."[54] For their part, many Muslims have come to see the conflict as having a strong religious element. Mustafa Ceric has described the war in his republic as "a kind of crusade against Islam and Muslims in Bosnia-Hercegovina," whose purpose was "to eliminate Islam and Muslims in this part of the world."[55] Earlier, when the war between Serbs and Croats still overshadowed the increasing tensions in Bosnia, Serbian Orthodox clergy had organized a news conference in Belgrade with the blunt title "The Religious War of the Vatican against the Orthodox Church."[56]

The simple assertion that the wars in the former Yugoslavia have had a religious basis is not, in itself, convincing proof that this is so. But there are other, more brutal forms of evidence. The large-scale, deliberate destruction of places of worship, religious schools, and even cemeteries—mostly by the Serbian side—is one indication of a religious motivation, even if that gained expression in the most negative way possible. Similarly, on a number of occasions the religious minority or the defeated communities recognized that their choice was to escape or convert to the religion of the victors; this dilemma strongly suggested that ethnoreligious hegemony was one of the perceived spoils of the conflict.[57]

But there is another side to this story. Under decades of communist rule, which was accompanied by the emergence of a modern industrialized society, the peoples of Yugoslavia had undergone a comprehensive process of secularization. This secularized Yugoslavia was hardly the ideal breeding ground for a religious conflict. It is also a curious coincidence that it should have been the Serbs who were the first to revive the ethnoreligious propaganda campaign and were then the most vociferous in attributing religious motivations to their Catholic and Muslim neighbors' alleged aggressiveness against Serbian Orthodoxy. Yet the Serbs are, by all accounts, the least religious of the three ethnic groups.

Nor has the conflict in Bosnia pitted only adherents of different faiths against each other. On the contrary, the Bosnian government has taken pride in having held together a multiethnic and multireligious alliance. It has included not only the Muslims but also sizeable minorities of the Serbian and Croatian communities, whose soldiers fought against their fellow nationals in the Bosnian Serb and Bosnian Croat forces. Muslims also fought each other after Fikret Abdic, a powerful Muslim leader in northwest Bosnia, broke away from the central government in 1993 and allied himself with the local Serbian forces until his defeat in the summer of 1995.

The conflict in the former Yugoslavia, as seen through the events of the first half of the 1990s, provides contradictory evidence on the importance of religion. Perhaps the safest conclusion to reach is that religion is so intrinsically bound up with nationalism in the region that its role cannot be ignored. Even if it is exploited by people with no religious beliefs, is misused for propaganda purposes, or is applied as a thin veneer to conceal other ulterior purposes, religion has been a component of the conflict that in recent years has torn countries, nations, and communities apart. That is not to argue, of course, that it has played a crucial part in triggering the wars and sustaining their destructive momentum. Much of the responsibility for that lies with an interplay of power struggles between regional elites that was sparked off by President Milosevic's drive to dominate the Yugoslav federation. In the battles that followed, the republican leaders whipped up and exploited the climate of interethnic enmities and fears—a combination that turned deadly when taking shape against the background of a serious economic crisis.

Many of these factors also represent a threat to stability elsewhere in the Balkans. The link between religion and nationalism remains strong in large areas of the region. For the former Yugoslav Republic of Macedonia its own Orthodox Church is a symbol of national independence. The failure of Greece and the new Yugoslavia of Serbia and Montenegro to recognize Macedonia's independence in the first half of the 1990s was reflected in their Orthodox churches' refusal to treat their Macedonian counterpart as an equal. Within rump-Yugoslavia, Montenegro's Orthodox faithful were formally split in 1993, when the supporters of Montenegro's independence from Serbia broke away from the Serbian Orthodox Church to reestablish their own autocephalous church. In Serbia's Kosovo province the restive local Albanian majority—mostly Muslim but with a small Catholic minority—have been at daggers-drawn with the Serbian Orthodox population.

Albanians are the major exception to the ethnoreligious homogeneity of the Balkans because within Albania the Muslim majority live side by side with Orthodox and Catholic minorities. Their relations have remained largely harmonious partly because Albanians do not regard religion as an integral part of their national identity. Yet even for Albania, religion represents a national problem because the country's Greek minority belongs to the Greek Orthodox Church, an institution many Albanians regard as carrying out a Hellenizing mission in their ranks. Some Albanians suspect that this mission is linked to Greek territorial claims to southern Albania, home to most of the country's ethnic Greeks.

Within Greece itself there has been a long-term tendency to cement the links between Greek national identity and the Orthodox Church while successive governments have been eager to break the ethnoreligious ties among their minority populations. Greece does not acknowledge that it has ethnic minorities such as the Turks. It simply regars them as Greeks of the Muslim faith.

The potential for an Orthodox-Muslim confrontation also exists in Bulgaria, where the Bulgarian Orthodox Church claims the allegiance of most of the country's religious population but the Turkish minority and a relatively small community of Slav Muslims, the Pomaks, belong to Islam. Under communist rule the government tried to eliminate the Turks as an ethnic minority and claimed that all Muslims in the country were of Bulgarian descent. But since the democratic transformation that started in late 1989, the Turkish minority has regained its status and its political party has at times even held the balance of power in parliament.

Further north, in Romania, ethnic tensions between Romanians and the Hungarian minority are also reflected in their different religious affiliations. The Romanians tend to belong to the Romanian Orthodox Church, while the ethnic Hungarians are split between the Catholic and the Reformed churches. The Romanian anticommunist revolution of 1989 gave a memorable example of interethnic and interreligious cooperation when it was triggered off by demonstrations in support of Laszlo Tokes, an ethnic Hungarian minister of the Reformed Church who was being persecuted by the secret police. But since then, Bishop Tokes has become a radical advocate of Hungarian minority rights, which many Romanians intensely dislike.

In the 1990s most Balkan countries have been going through a painful process of transformation. In a number of states the transition from communism to a market economy, from one-party rule to democracy, has been accomplished, although in some cases with only a moderate degree of success. In other, war-torn countries, the attempt has met with profound failure. But in almost every instance the transition has been accompanied by a revival of nationalism. In the Balkans, nationalism has for long been closely intertwined with religion. Although over the past half-century the role of religion has been much reduced by the emergence of largely secular societies, the renewed nationalist fervor of the 1990s has given a new lease on life to religion. Although religion may not be among the main causes behind the tragedy of Yugoslavia, in its alliance with nationalism it remains a potent force that can, in some cases, exacerbate the multiplicity of ethnic conflicts in the Balkans.

Notes

I am very grateful to Branka Magas and Cornelia Sorabji for their valuable comments on an earlier version of this article.

1. For the purposes of brevity, Bosnia-Hercegovina will be referred to as Bosnia throughout this chapter.

2. This brief historical outline is based on Stella Alexander, *Church and State in Yugoslavia since 1945* (Cambridge: Cambridge University Press, 1979); Robert J. Donia and John V. A. Fine, Jr., *Bosnia and Hercegovina: A Tradition Betrayed* (London: Hurst and Co., 1994); Noel Malcolm, *Bosnia: A Short History*, rev. ed. (London: Papermac, 1996); Stevan K. Pavlowitch, *The Improbable Survivor: Yugoslavia and Its Problems, 1918–1988* (London: Hurst and Co., 1988); Pedro Ramet, "Religion and Nationalism in Yugoslavia" in *Religion and Nationalism in Soviet and East European Politics* (Durham, NC: Duke University Press, 1984), pp. 149–69; Zachary T. Irwin, "The Fate of Islam in the Balkans" in *Religion and Nationalism in Soviet and East European Politics*, ed. Pedro Ramet (Durham, NC: Duke University Press, 1984), pp. 207–25; Sabrina Petra Ramet, *Balkan Babel: Politics, Culture, and Religion in Yugoslavia* (Boulder, Colo.: Westview Press, 1992).

3. Associated Press (AP) report, 15 February 1992.

4. The role of the Catholic and Orthodox Churches in the origins and early phase of the fighting in the former Yugoslavia is discussed by Geert van Dartel, "The Nations and Churches in Yugoslavia," *Religion, State and Society* 20 (1992): pp. 275–88, and by Paul Mojzes in "The Role of the Religious Communities in the War in Former Yugoslavia," *Religion in Eastern Europe* 13, (June 1993): pp. 13–31, which the author updated and expanded in his *Yugoslavian Inferno: Ethnoreligious Warfare in the Balkans* (New York: Continuum, 1994). A comprehensive post-Dayton assessment of religion during the years of conflict is provided in *War Report: Bulletin of the Institute for War and Peace Reporting* no. 40 (April 1996), pp. 20–38, a special feature with contributions by Gabriel Partos, Srdjan Vrcan, Mirko Djordjevic, Smail Balic, Gojko Beric, Jaroslav Pecnik, and Anton Berishaj.

5. Keston News Service (KNS), report no. 345, 8 March 1990, p. 14.

6. *Independent* (London), 31 May 1990.

7. KNS, no. 357, 30 August 1990, p. 11, and no. 379, 11 July 1991, p. 6.

8. *Guardian*, 6 November 1991.

9. *Observer* (London), 29 December 1991, quoting Robert Schretter.

10. *Guardian*, 6 November 1991, quoting Antun Ivanisa.

11. Reuters, 21 June 1994.

12. *Tablet* (London), 11 September 1993, quoting Fr. Peter.

13. Ibid., 17 July 1993.   14. Ibid.
15. *Independent*, 8 August 1994.   16. Reuters, 1 October 1995.
17. KNS, no. 355, 26 July 1990, p. 12, quoting *Pravoslavlje*, 1 July 1990.
18. Ibid., no. 369, 21 February 1991, p. 18.
19. Ibid., no. 261, 25 October 1991, p. 11.
20. *Politika*, 26 October 1991.
21. AP, 15 February 1992.
22. Agence France Presse (AFP), 16 March, quoting *Vecernje Novosti*.
23. Gordon N. Bardos, "The Serbian Church against Milosevic," *Radio Free Europe/Radio Liberty [RFE/RL] Research Report*, 13 July 1992, p. 8, quoting *Pravoslavlje*.
24. KNS, no. 364, 6 December 1990.
25. *Summary of World Broadcasts (SWB)*, EE/2072 C/2, 12 August 1994, quoting *Tanjug*, 10 August 1994.
26. *Guardian*, 17 August 1995; AP, 7 August 1995.
27. *SWB*, EE/1408 C1/3 16 June 1992, quoting *Tanjug*, 14 June 1992.
28. Ibid., EE/1665 C1/8. 7 April 1993, quoting *Tanjug*, 15 April 1993.
29. Reuters, 27 January 1994.
30. AFP, 8 January 1996; AP, 9 January 1996; AFP, 13 March 1996.
31. The recent role of Islam in the Balkans is discussed by H. T. Norris in his paper, "Muslim Dreams and Tensions within the Balkans: A Pending Struggle between the Heart of European Islam and a 'Craze with the Spell of Far Arabia,'" presented at a conference on Semantics and Security: The Meaning of the Balkans, at the School of Slavonic and East European Studies, University of London, 23 September 1994.
32. "The Trial of Muslim Intellectuals in Sarajevo" (*The Islamic Declaration*), *South Slav Journal* 6, no. 1 (1983): p. 76.
33. *Guardian*, 27 December 1993.   34. *Tablet*, 31 July 1993.
35. *Guardian*, 26 June 1993.   36. KNS, 27 June 1991, p. 12.
37. *Times* (London), 14 January 1992.
38. Ibid., 8 August 1992.
39. Reuters, 23 January 1994; AFP, 23 July 1995.
40. *International Herald Tribune (IHT)*, 6 September 1994.
41. Ibid., 12 September 1994.
42. *SWB*, EE/2096 C/3, 9 September 1994, quoting Croatian Radio, 7 September 1994.
43. Itar-Tass news agency, 17 August 1996.
44. *SWB*, SU/2124 B/12, 12 October 1994, quoting Interfax news agency, 10 October 1994.
45. *A Report on the Devastation of Cultural, Historical and Natural Heritage of the Republic/Federation of Bosnia and Hercegovina, from April 5, 1992 until September 5, 1995* (Sarajevo: Institute for Protection of Cultural, Historical and Natural Heritage of the Republic of Bosnia and Hercegovina, 1995); letter to author from the State Authority for the Protection of Cultural and Natural Heritage, Republic of Croatia; *Vecernji list*, 1 October 1995; *SWB*, quoting *Tanjug*, 14 June 1993; Reuters, 15 May 1994.
46. *Independent on Sunday*, 19 June 1994.
47. Sabrina Petra Ramet, *Balkan Babel: Politics, Culture and Religion in Yugoslavia* (Boulder, Colo.: Westview Press, 1992), p. 140; *SWB*, EE/8283/B6, 12 June 1986, quoting *Tanjug*, 8 June 1986.
48. *Guardian*, 6 November 1991.

49. *European* (London), 22 July 1993.
50. *SWB*, EE/2291 C/11, quoting IRNA news agency, 29 April 1995.
51. *Guardian Weekly*, 8 April 1994, quoting *Le Monde*, 27–28 March 1994.
52. Reuters, 30 September 1994.
53. Ibid., 9 October 1994; *IHT*, 17 November 1994.
54. Patrick Moore, "The Islamic Community's New Sense of Identity," *RFE: Report on Eastern Europe*, 1 November 1991, p. 21, quoting *Middle East*, October 1991.
55. Reuters, 16 May 1994.
56. *SWB*, EE/1335 C1.5, 21 March 1992, quoting *Tanjug*, 19 March 1992.
57. *Independent on Sunday*, 19 June 1994.

: 6 :

Multiculturalism, Religious Conservatism, and American Diversity

Nathan Glazer

Multiculturalism and diversity seem to be ruling themes in American culture today. The term *diversity* crops up everywhere on the American campus: Students, faculty and administrators are to be sensitive to diversity; dormitory residents seem to require training in diversity; the composition of the student body, faculty, and administration should reflect American diversity, and the curriculum should reflect it too. Others also require training in diversity and in the sensitivity necessary to deal with diversity: newspaper reporters, administrators of employees in any institution, personnel managers anywhere. *Multiculturalism* has an even wider usage. Even if its first and principal use is in education, we find it now everywhere, referring to a policeman who can deal with people of various backgrounds ("Multicultural Cop," reads one headline) as well as to food and dress. Richard Bernstein tells us that the term *multicultural* or *multiculturalism* appeared in forty newspaper articles in 1980 but in two thousand articles in 1992.[1] *Diversity* would probably show a similar rise.

Conservative religion also appears more prominently in public discourse today. While it seems directly opposed to the kind of pluralism advocated by proponents of multiculturalism, conservative religion also raises divisive issues in American life and politics, as we see from the debates over abortion, sex education, prayer in schools, and other social issues that engage the question of diversity of life-style and moral practice. In this chapter, I discuss the significance of this upsurge in concern for diversity and multiculturalism, its relation to the new prominence of religious conservatism, and what it means for American society.

The "New" Diversity

Diversity in its current usage seems to encompass primarily diversity in race, ethnicity, and gender. It also refers to differences based on what is now called sexual orientation (i.e., being gay or lesbian) and in lesser degree to other kinds of diversity, such as that caused by physical impairment or age. Its primary reference, however, is to diversity of race and ethnicity, with gender playing almost as large a role.

Historical perspective is useful in considering the rise of a new term, and perhaps the first thing to be noted here are the differences that diversity does *not* currently refer to but that would have been primary if the question of differences among Americans were being discussed two hundred years ago or one hundred years ago or fifty years ago. In earlier periods we would have had in mind, when we considered differences among Americans, differences of religion or differences in region and occupation (e.g., whether one was a Northerner or a Southerner, a farmer or merchant). In the 1930s differences of class and occupation would have been decisive—whether one was a worker or employer, a debtor or a lender, a sharecropper or a farm owner.

Obviously, none of these differences has disappeared. But their significance has been somewhat reduced in the public mind—particularly in schools, colleges, and universities—in contrast with differences of race and ethnicity. In the Kennedy School of Government at Harvard University, for example, one can find a host of bulletin boards addressed to students of different ethnic and racial groups, to women and gays and lesbians, each displayed by an organization of students of that group, but there are no bulletin boards for religious groups or regional groups. Why class differences and religious and regional differences, which have played so large a role in American society, do not first come to mind when speaking of multiculturalism or diversity today is an interesting question. Economic differences are always crucial in a society; religious differences in American society not only remain salient but have increased in significance in some respects in the past two decades. As more and more Americans are concerned with what seems like a collapse in traditional morality, as reflected in a great rise in births out of wedlock, widespread use of drugs, and more crime and imprisonment, conservative religious groups have become more prominent and more powerful in American politics.

The issues they raise—the legal status of abortion, the role of prayer in schools, what values should be taught in schools—may not have much to do with the change in the moral climate, but they have become permanent and abrasive subjects of conflict in American society. Abortion became a national issue when the Supreme Court declared state limitations on abortion unconstitutional, a decision that gave rise to a powerful antiabortion movement, primarily religion-based. This movement has protested the decision for decades, by measures becoming ever more forceful and spilling over recently into violence and assassinations of abortion doctors. There has been a similar battle over the legitimacy of prayer or its substitutes (e.g., a moment of silence) in public schools, following sharply restrictive Supreme Court decisions. An amendment to the Constitution that would reinstate school prayer to some degree has found a good deal of support in Congress. These issues, too, raise questions of diversity, even if we think of race and ethnicity first in speaking today of American diversity.

These issues are not new on the American scene. Race and ethnicity have been intertwined with the major controversies of American public life from the beginning. Blacks are the chief group we have in mind when we speak of diversity today: They are the largest American minority (12 percent), and they and their fate have played a key role in American history. Slavery and its aftermath was the dominant single fact of American political life for a good part of its history. Chinese and Japanese immigration in the second half of the nineteenth century aroused racial antagonisms almost as strong as those that Blacks encountered. This led to the first sharp restrictions in American immigration in the late nineteenth and early twentieth centuries. The shift in the European sources of American immigration, from northern and western Europe to southern and eastern Europe, was a chief subject of public concern between the 1890s and the 1920s and led to sharp restrictions in American immigration in the 1920s that were in place until 1965. The situation of Blacks has been the single most important domestic issue in American life for the past forty years at least.

If we had been using the term *diversity* one hundred years ago, we would have had in mind religion, even before race and ethnicity. The United States was an overwhelmingly Protestant society—of many denominations—as well as an overwhelmingly White society. Catholics and Jews often faced discrimination, and even in the absence of discrimination they thought of themselves as minorities with little power. That has changed: formal religious affiliation is less important today as a basis of division or discrimination than it has been through most of American history. But as I indicated above, key conflicts based on religion have increased in importance in recent decades. These conflicts are not based, as those in the past were, on differences among Catholics, Protestants, and Jews. The denominations get along better today than in the past. But in each major religious grouping there are sharp divisions between liberals and progressives, on the one hand, and fundamentalists and conservatives on the other. These divisions determine whether one has religious objections to abortion or teaching about sex in schools or—the issue is still a potent one in some school districts and states—whether one teaches evolution as "theory" or "fact."

While we have in mind today when we use the term *diversity* principally ethnic and racial groups, one group dominates in our consideration of diversity: Blacks, or African Americans, with the preferred term now shifting rapidly from the former to the latter. We also have in mind, but not as prominently, the second largest "minority," as we use that term today, Hispanics, with the preferred term shifting to Latinos. But the diversity among Latinos—Puerto Ricans, Mexicans, Cubans, Dominicans, Salvadorans, Nicaraguans, Colombians, Ecuadorans, and others—is such that different groups raise different issues, and they do not present the one big issue that African Americans have always presented in American life. Different groups of Hispanics have rather different interests and concerns. Cubans worry about our policy toward Castro; Mexicans, about how we will handle illegal immigration; Puerto Ricans, about high rates in the ranks of the poor and the welfare population; Nicaraguans and Salvadorans, about the future of our refugee and asylum policies. Latinos are scarcely a group unified by common issues and concerns, but they may become such.

We also have in mind when we speak of diversity the oldest American minority, American Indians, now increasingly referred to as Native Americans. But if one considers numbers alone (African Americans, 12 percent; Hispanics, 8 percent; Native Americans, 1 percent), not to mention other factors such as salience in American politics, it is African Americans who dominate in discussions of American diversity.

Asian Americans are a rising percentage of the American population, doubling to more than 3 percent of the American population between 1980 and 1990 but already 10 percent in California and sure to show a greater percentage increase by the year 2000 than any other group. Despite diversity greater than that which characterizes Hispanics and Latinos—Asians include Chinese and Japanese, Filipinos and Vietnamese, Asian Indians, Bangladeshis, Pakistanis, and many more—they are now regularly combined and listed among American minorities, and as a rising new term has it, they are also "people of color." When we create a category of Americans that are "minorities" or "of color," we assume that all these groups have common problems, owing primarily to the fact that they have suffered from discrimination in the past and in varying degrees still do in the present and that a prevailing racism in the American mind has placed all nonwhite peoples in this common inferior category. This is why, when affirmative action first came on the scene in the late 1960s, the groups to which employers and contractors were to pay particular attention (they could not, of course, under law, discriminate against anyone on the basis of race or ethnicity), the specifically "protected groups" included the four racial groups, or congeries of groups, I have discussed: Blacks, Hispanics, American Indians, and Asians.

There were from the beginning anomalies in lumping them in a common category as groups suffering especially from discrimination. Cubans, for example, received preference from the American government in gaining admission to the United States and in access to government benefits, and Asians were already at the level of the American population in general, or ahead, in education, income, and representation in preferred occupations and professions. Nevertheless, non-White or non-European origins appeared to the policymakers of the time as a good basis on which to set up categories that had some claim to a special degree of protection by government from racial and group discrimination. These anomalies have increased over time. Cubans now dominate the politics and economy of southern Florida; Asians have increased their advantage in higher education, making up 20 percent or more of the enrollment in our elite colleges or universities (recall they are only 3 percent of the population); and it is generally accepted that English-speaking Black immigrants from the Caribbean have an economic and educational advantage over native American Blacks. A program originally designed to make up for discrimination against American minorities now offers benefits to groups the majority of whom were not even resident in this country when the affirmative action program was devised. But no one in the late 1960s was thinking of the new waves of immigration that would be generated by the immigration reform act of 1965.

It is very hard to change official categories once they have been established and once they become fixed categories in the public mind and in public action, however inappropriately. It would be enormously difficult politically for the federal government to declare that there is no longer any reason to consider Asians a minority that requires the distinctive protection of affirmative action. In fact, they no longer get such preference in college admissions—more likely the reverse—nor in employment, but they are still reported in the statistics colleges and universities and employers must provide to demonstrate their diversity or nondiscrimination. The one aspect of affirmative action that interests Asian Americans and that they would not surrender without a fight is preference in bidding on government contracts, the kind of preference that, in various jurisdictions, Blacks, Hispanics, American Indians, and women receive.

There are other potential benefits to being considered an aggrieved minority entitled to special consideration. A group of Asian American students at Harvard once asked me to participate in a program on the question "Are Asians a minority?" What was the issue, I asked. Certainly they were a numerical minority (who is not in the United States?), but clearly something else was on their minds. It seemed there were foundation-funded fellowships administered by the university to encourage minorities to enter doctoral programs in the humanities; but when Asian students applied for these fellowships, they discovered that they were not included among the minorities this program was intended to benefit. They had been dropped from the preferred list of those deserving special consideration because of past discrimination. This made sense to me. Even if Asians were not overrepresented as professors in the humanities, they were certainly overrepresented overall on college faculties, and the fellowship program was clearly intended for underrepresented minorities, primarily Blacks. This did not please the Asian students.

Asians may be considered honorary members of the groups people have in mind when they discuss diversity and minorities. They are the least problematic minority or persons of color; they are, indeed, the model minority, as one term has it. They do well educationally and economically on the whole, have strong families, do not appear disproportionately on the welfare rolls or in the ranks of criminals. Asian spokesmen object to the term "model minority," while they simultaneously take pride in the achievement that has earned them this appellation. But they do not want to give up any possible claims based on past or present discrimination either.

Even less at issue than Asians are European ethnic groups. They were also once minorities and used to be regularly included in sociology textbooks on American minorities. Indeed, Jews may well be considered the universal minority, as they were before the establishment of the state of Israel. Nevertheless, when we speak about diversity and multiculturalism in the United States today, we do not generally have Jews, Italians, Poles, Irish, or any other European group in mind. As late as the 1970s, in an earlier burst of multiculturalism, when centers were being established for Black and other ethnic studies, Jews, Italians, and some other European-origin groups made claims that they should have their ethnic studies centers too. But it was soon clear that the assimilation of these groups had progressed so far and discrimination against them had become so minor that these groups soon dropped out of concern and out of mind when issues of diversity and multiculturalism came up.

Immigration and Multiculturalism

You will not find much argument about diversity in American discourse today. Everyone considers it a good thing. Our immigration runs at about one million a year and contributes mightily to diversity—90 percent of it is Black, Asian, and Latin American, whereas only 25 percent of the country is made up of these groups. Yet it is only very recently that we have heard any suggestion that we should change our immigration policies to increase the number of Europeans, the origins of three-quarters of Americans, or that it would be legitimate for immigration policy to attempt to reflect the present racial-ethnic balance of the population. That is still for the most part off-limits in public discussion. It would remind people of the racist and anti-Catholic and anti-Jewish immigration policies we adopted in the 1920s, which were specifically based on the principle that immigration should reflect the ethnic composition of the existing American population. In 1995, Peter Brimelow, who is himself a British immigrant, raised this issue of the changing racial-ethnic composition of American immigration in his book *Alien Nation*, but this was fiercely attacked.

The major debate about immigration until 1994 was limited to the question of what to do about illegal immigration. The debate was greatly broadened with the Republican congressional victory of 1994. In the welfare legislation prepared in Congress during the autumn of 1995, legal immigrants and legal immigrant students were slated to lose some benefits. The proposed legislation would require that the income of the person who had sponsored the immigrant be considered part of the immigrant's assets in assessing eligibility for welfare, student aid, and other benefits. An important referendum in California in 1994 eliminated all state benefits to illegal immigrants, and this may be imitated in other states, but the constitutionality of the California restriction has been challenged in federal court and may not be sustained. In any case, legal immigrants were not affected by the California vote.

Nevertheless, while almost no one opposes diversity and the increasing diversity that is an effect of our immigration policies, many oppose multiculturalism, which is a way of recognizing and responding to diversity.

What do we mean by multiculturalism? In the broadest sense, it is the argument that American diversity is characterized by subcultures that encompass various ethnic and racial groups, as well as women and groups defined on some other bases (in particular, homosexuality), and that these subcultures have been unfairly ignored and denigrated in American public life. This public life has been characterized, multicultural critics charge, by an assumption of homogeneity in American culture. It unfairly imposes on all respect for the same national heroes and common national holidays and observances and an education concentrating uniquely on a single story in American history, the story of the English founders of the Atlantic colonies. This story ignores all other ethnic and racial strands in the making of America and is further limited by dealing only with the males among these presumed founders and their descendants. So from a multicultural point of view we should recognize, for example, that American Indians are a distinct and separate group, as are American Blacks and the variants of American Hispanics and Asian Americans, each with its own story, largely one of victimization by Whites but in each case including important contributions to American life.

The term *multiculturalism* has also been expanded to include women as a group, with not only special interests but distinct cultural characteristics, in a sense a subculture. This is by now so well established that there are hundreds of women's studies programs in American colleges and universities and scores of courses on women's issues and gender issues in departments of English, anthropology, sociology, and elsewhere. Indeed, a women's perspective informs a good part of the curriculum in the humanities and the social sciences today. It is scarcely to be found, however, in the sciences, though some feminists argue that there is or should be such a perspective.

The meaning of multiculturalism is also now expanding to encompass the distinct subcultural characteristics of homosexuals, and in many universities there are nascent programs in gay and lesbian studies; in some, fully developed programs. The Brown University catalog for 1993–1994, as a student from Brown in the Salzburg Seminar on diversity in the summer of 1994 informed me, included such courses in the departments of American studies ("Identities/Communities: Queer Cultures in Theory, History, and Politics"), English ("Unspeakable Desires," "Queer Theory"), and undoubtedly other fields. The inclusion of discussion of gay and lesbian families in a proposed multicultural curriculum for the New York City elementary and high schools led to an uproar that forced the resignation of the chancellor of the public schools.

Multiculturalism is an issue that comes up in all sectors of American life today, but disputes have been most intense in the area of education. Perhaps the first shot in the current conflict was fired at Stanford University, where some minority students, joined by liberal faculty, objected to a required course in classics of Western civilization. Why only *Western* classics, it was asked. Why did it deal only with work by males, white males? This criticism was satirized by the defenders of the traditional courses in Western classics: the multiculturalists, they said, were on the warpath against work by DWMs (dead white males) even though these were the central classics of the Western tradition. This conflict on one American campus was widely reported and commented on in the press. It ended in compromise but a compromise in which, to use another widely noted phrase in the dispute over multiculturalism, works introducing themes of "class, race, and gender," written by authors who themselves belonged to subordinate classes, races, and genders, were to supplement a reduced list of Western classics.

This was different from the argument over Black studies and ethnic studies in the 1970s. These older forms of recognition only gave Blacks and other ethnic groups a place in the array of departmental specializations. At Stanford the demand was that everyone must be exposed to the multicultural aspect of American life. Multiculturalism, as in the new required course, was for everyone.

The dispute has been repeated in many other institutions, with variations. At the University of California in Berkeley, which did not have required courses similar to the one in Western civilization at Stanford, the issue raised by multiculturalists was that there should be a required course that dealt with the leading American minorities. In the battle within the faculty, the traditionalists were able to get European-Americans included as one of the groups that could be covered, along with Blacks, Latinos, Asian Americans, and Native Americans, in courses that fulfilled this new multicultural requirement. A committee was established to which faculty would submit course proposals for approval in meeting the required guidelines. This became the only universally required course at the University of California, Berkeley. At Hunter College in New York City, at the University of Minnesota, and elsewhere more than one multicultural course was required of students. One required course, it is asserted in many institutions, is not enough; there should be a second.

The argument over multiculturalism in the public schools has been more serious than the argument in colleges and universities. Colleges and universities are various: among three thousand institutions of higher education one can find many, I am sure, that have resisted the multicultural tidal wave. Further, even where such courses are required, one or two in a college curriculum that might include forty courses may not be an unbearable imposition. But one has much less opportunity to choose one's elementary or high school: in the public systems that 90 percent of Americans attend, one is almost universally assigned to a school, with very limited choice. Further, public school curricula are in measure publicly prescribed and are set for all students, whether they attend private or public schools. Legislatures may require that all students be exposed to certain material. (It has become popular recently, for example, to require some instruction on the Holocaust.) For the public elementary and high schools, publicly appointed bodies set a curriculum; textbooks may be approved, and all students may be taught from these publicly approved texts. While in the United States we are far from a French- or Japanese-style curricular uniformity, within given states we may approach the norms of these more centralized states. In the public schools we deal with curricula prescribed for all, which none may escape, designed by public bodies. It is no wonder the battles are as intense over multicultural issues in the public schools as in the colleges.

The issues that are being debated in the dispute over multiculturalism involve more than education in a narrow sense and are of much wider interest and importance than other debates involving schools, colleges, and curricula. Multiculturalism raises the question of American identity— what it is, how it is to be inculcated in our children and in the million immigrants a year who become part of the United States, what are the limits to which it can be stretched before some vague but unpleasant consequences follow. The issue has become so important because it arises against a background in which "assimilation" to an American identity was taken for granted as an objective of public policy—and not only educational policy—and assimilation was in large measure successfully implemented. When an ideal that was accepted as legitimate and essential is radically challenged, as multiculturalism challenges assimilation, discomfort at least will be felt; and more than discomfort, fervid opposition can be expected.

The fate of assimilation is the central issue that animates the debate over multiculturalism. Just what was intended or expected from immigrants in the heyday of assimilation is not absolutely clear. It meant certainly that old national loyalties should be expunged. It meant also that the United States was to be accepted by all its citizens as a kind of paragon among nations, and so our patriotic songs, our Pledge of Allegiance, our national holidays and ceremonies all celebrated the distinctive virtue of the United States.

Just what that virtue consisted of would change over the years. A central place in defining it was taken by the Declaration of Independence and the Constitution. They celebrated the somewhat contradictory principles of liberty and equality. Seymour Martin Lipset, among others, has argued that these two principles seem to alternate in dominating American life and politics.[2] But in emphasizing principles, values, and ideals that were divorced from one exclusive ethnic base and by downplaying the notion that some primordial connection bound together all the American people, the American polity took on a distinctive character, rather more open to incorporating people from various ethnic backgrounds than were others. After all, the Constitution itself presumed that many Americans would be immigrants born abroad and reserved only the position of president to the native-born. It gave to Congress the specific right to "establish an uniform rule of naturalization."

It is undoubtedly true that the founding fathers did not expect prospective Americans to come from areas very different from those from which the existing Americans of the late eighteenth century had come—

the British Isles and northwestern Europe. When Crèvecoeur wrote his famous response to the question he had set himself in 1782, "What then is the American, this new man?" he celebrated the diversity of American origins, but by present-day standards they were not very diverse. The American, he wrote, "is either a European or the descendant of a European, hence that strange mixture of blood, which you will find in no other country. I could point out to you a family whose grandfather was an Englishman, whose wife was Dutch, whose son married a French woman, and whose present four sons have four wives of four different nations. *He* is an American, who, leaving behind him all his ancient prejudices and manners, receives new ones from the new mode of life he has embraced, the new government he obeys, and the new rank he holds." Philip Gleason writes that this passage "has probably been quoted more than any other in the history of immigration."[3] But what would strike us today would be less its expansiveness than its restriction to Europeans.

Nevertheless, the implicit framework for steady expansion of the ideas of who could legitimately become an American existed in the principles of the Declaration and the Constitution and became explicit in the post–Civil War amendments. Even this did not settle the matter: Blacks could not achieve the equality these amendments granted them for one hundred years after they were adopted; Chinese and Japanese were excluded from immigration and citizenship; and the immigration restriction laws of the 1920s, which prevailed until 1965, sharply limited immigration from eastern and southern Europe and banned immigration from Asia entirely.

Furthermore, these ethnic and racial restrictions coexisted with an expectation of, a demand for, assimilation. This could be seen as narrow and overbearing, and it was; but it also had another aspect—welcome and incorporation. Immigrants were expected to become Americans. They were expected to become citizens and learn English. Socially, they might find prejudice and discrimination, but in public law and ceremony they found acceptance. This acceptance offered no accommodation to their original languages, cultures, and loyalties, but immigrants on the whole accepted the bargain and offered no resistance to it. After the 1960s the welcome became worldwide. By 1986, when the Statue of Liberty was rededicated, it had changed in its symbolic meaning for the United States. The original name of the statue was "Liberty Enlightening the World." It had now become a statue of Lady Liberty welcoming the immigrants.

In the light of this history, this expectation of assimilation, multiculturalism comes as a shock. Multiculturalism in almost all its aspects gives no special credit to European origins nor to the English origins of American governmental principles. But if assimilation is not to be the goal of the various groups that make up America and of the non-White and non-

European groups now increasing in number through immigration, what is the alternative? The fear is that the alternative is not an orchestra of diversity in harmony but a discordant medley of conflicting voices, each making claims on the basis of a history of distinctive victimization. The critics of multiculturalism raise the specter of Canada, on the verge of separation into two countries over the past few decades, or even worse, of the former Yugoslavia. It is this background and this prospect that gives such intensity to the debate over multiculturalism.

What role does conflict over religion play in the conflicts over multiculturalism? Multicultural issues and religious issues often seem to operate along separate tracks, but they do intersect. The multicultural advocates who represent minorities call for more attention to their history, their oppression, their presence, their contribution. These are not matters that much concern religious conservatives, nor are they matters on which they would come into direct conflict with multiculturalists, even though the religious conservatives clearly find nothing much wrong with the traditional schools and curricula of the 1950s and before. On the other hand, when it comes to the demands of the new nonminority "identity groups" that also play a major role in multicultural conflicts—that is, feminists and homosexual life-style defenders—direct conflict does occur.

For example, a new proposed New York City curriculum teaching about different family life-styles, seen by many as an attempt to place the family composed of a homosexual couple on the same moral footing as the traditional two-parent family, aroused fierce conflict in New York City. Conservative and fundamentalist religious groups oppose explicit sex education in public elementary and secondary schools, including instruction in the use of condoms, which is advocated by homosexual groups on the ground this is necessary to combat the spread of AIDS. The religious conservatives find the acknowledgment of homosexual life-styles repugnant. Thus, when the National Education Association (NEA), the largest teachers union, under the pressure of one wing of multiculturalists, passed a resolution in favor of a Lesbian and Gay History Month, it was attacked by conservative groups, and some members of the NEA resigned for religious reasons.[4] Feminist groups favor—and conservative religious figures oppose—curricular materials that break down the traditional separation between male and female roles, showing the man as housekeeper and child rearer, the woman at work in traditionally male occupations.

Thus, we find two assaults on the modal public schools of our day, which are blandly liberal and eschew moral instruction, by multiculturalists and conservative religionists. They are quite separate and often opposed in their motivations and intentions and in their impact on the schools. To the liberal center that dominates public education the demands of the multiculturalists make sense and have been widely accepted. It is true that liberals devoted to universal principles of truth-seeking and color-blindness, such as Arthur Schlesinger Jr., have been strong opponents of multiculturalism, but the stronger opponents are found among political conservatives. Liberals, including those who oppose multiculturalism, are more alarmed by the assault of religious conservatives, with their battle cries of prayer in the schools, traditional values in the curriculum, and at the extreme, resistance to the teaching of evolution as contradictory of the biblical account of creation.

There is widespread alarm over what these two movements of the discontented may do to American life, politics, and culture, but the alarm is felt by different groups. Liberal and secular elements fear the impact of religion on American life and education; nationalist Americans of all stripes, liberal and conservative, fear the effect of the multicultural assault. Both movements have already led to change. As I indicated above, curricula in higher education have already undergone great changes as a result of multicultural demands. Textbooks have been altered in elementary and secondary schools to give greater attention to racial and ethnic groups and women. Religious organizations have been more powerful in Congress and in public opinion than in colleges and schools; there a secular and liberal spirit prevails, and it is the multicultural demands that are more powerful and effective.

Assimilation and Its Opponents

Many Americans fear the traditional American capacity to assimilate new groups is failing as a result of the rise of multiculturalism. But as far as new immigrant groups are concerned, I believe America's traditionally strong assimilatory effects are still at work. It is not the new immigrants who are the chief proponents of multiculturalism. The most vigorous voices for multiculturalism are to be found in the Black community and among women. Just as immigrants accepted assimilation and "Americanization" in the past, even when this was insensitively imposed on them, so I believe they accept it today. More than simply passively accepting assimilation and Americanization, many immigrants in the past actively pursued it and not only for practical advantages: they wanted to actively change their identities, to become Americans. I believe the same is true for many today.

But there was in fact one enormous failure in the program for assimilation. African Americans, among the first settlers in the English colonies (even if not willingly), were basically excluded from the process of assimilation, whether defined politically to include the full panoply of citizenship rights or socially or culturally. It is therefore not surprising that the strongest voices for multiculturalism, those who go furthest in developing this as a program for the schools and colleges and in all relevant spheres of American life, are African Americans. Not all, by far, have joined the multiculturalist crusade and its specifically African American variant, Afrocentrism. Despite the distinctive, almost unique rejection African Americans found in American society, many Black intellectuals are ardent and eloquent in insisting that all they want is full rights as Americans and participation in American society on terms of full equality. But it would be no surprise if many responded to the long history of exclusion by asserting, as James Baldwin once put it, that they did not want to be integrated into a burning house, that they would insist on recovering, fostering, and expanding a culture of their own.

There is an odd asymmetry between the sources of the demands for multiculturalism and the fears that it arouses. Its sources, I believe, are largely the great American failure, the great American dilemma—the failure to fully incorporate Blacks. Blacks show even today a unique pattern of residential segregation, a distinctively low rate of intermarriage with other Americans—and residential integration and intermarriage are two of the best measures of assimilation. The strongest fears multiculturalism arouses are of a national disunity, even a breakup, parallel to what we see in other multinational states. But that is not what we should fear. When it comes to culture and language, American assimilatory trends are as strong as they ever were. Our problem is not the problem of a nascent Quebec or of Croatians, Bosnians, and Serbians at each other's throats. It is at bottom the problem of the full incorporation of Blacks into American society. The various Asian groups will find their way into the American polity and society, and I believe most of the Latino groups will. Immigration is a problem, but it is for most immigrants the same kind of problem of adaptation that it has been in the past. It brings its discomforts, some of them severe, but it does not portend by itself a more divided society. An older American problem does.

By emphasizing the importance of the history and situation of African Americans, as against immigrants, in the rise of multiculturalism, I do not mean to suggest that there are no other elements that have contributed to multicultural demands and programs. We could not explain the strength of the aspects of multiculturalism that respond to the concerns of women and of gays and lesbians by reference to the problems of Blacks. There are other —perhaps larger—forces at work in creating something of an "identity explosion." This seems to be connected with criticism of some failures of our advanced Western civilization and even criticism of elements of Western

...essful and least challenge-
...ments of science itself).

...icultural explosion, includ-
...irtues of the United States
...al, and economic predomi-
...War II could not have been
...reat trauma of the war, but
...), specific worsening prob-
...ner-city decay), and specific
...e. All of these have shaken

...e to the United States, seem
...ld not explain why one finds
...ralia, the United Kingdom,
...distinctive American experi-
...nd self-confident view of our
...only the United States but the
advanced countries of Europe, too, that do not handle problems as well as
they believed they did in the 1950s and 1960s. The power of the developed
Western states no longer permits easy answers to difficult international
issues, their science and technology raises unexpected problems, and their
confidence in inevitable progress is for these and other reasons weakened.

Multiculturalism has its distinctive American causes and motors. But it
is more than American problems that leads to the new "identity politics."
Perhaps it is the basic Western commitment to liberty and equality that creates the circumstances that lead to an internal criticism of our Western societies. The societies that have given the greatest weight to the values of liberty and equality are hoist by their own petard. Why, their critics ask, does
liberty and equality extend only to the isolated individual, why not liberty
for groups to pursue their own cultures, equality in their ability to do so?
Equality turns out to be a boundless value. If one has political equality,
the question will come up, why not economic equality? If equality is available to all men, why are there distinctive occupations, statuses, and behaviors limited to some? If equality is available to all, why not equality for
gays and lesbians, for the handicapped in all possible ways? The political
value of liberty assures that these and many other demands will be raised;
government under law assures there will be ways to raise them effectively.

The explosion of ethnic identities in so many countries—belying expectations, whether liberal or radical or capitalist, that these would be super-
seded by identities based on class or occupation or income—shows that
identity politics is more than an American problem. But of course, in each

country it will take a different form, depending on its history and problems. In the United States that distinctive form is most strongly shaped by the problem of a full and equal incorporation of Blacks into American society, an effort in which we have made great strides and great progress but where substantial success still eludes us. Because of that problem the assimilationist ideal and program seems inadequate, even hypocritical, and something else seems demanded. Multiculturalism is a crude and still-evolving response to that failure.

We are equally unclear as to what the other assault of the discontented on centrist American liberalism—the assault of fundamentalist and conservative religious groups—means for American society and polity. The conservative Christian movement claims it is trying to restore a better world. (The multiculturalists by contrast do not hark back to a better America; they see the better America as that which will emerge as a result of their demands.) But the opponents of the Christian movement see a dangerous disregard for law, as enshrined in the Constitution, and its interpretation by the Supreme Court. Here too the public school and the college and university are central arenas for conflict. May the Ten Commandments be placed on the school walls? (Martin Luther King and Malcolm X are already there.) May prayers be conducted at graduations? May conservative Christian groups have the same rights to organize, to get college or university funds, to proselytize, as do the various ethnic and racial and sex-orientation groups that proliferate on campus? May single-sex institutions, such as the Virginia Military Institute, be allowed to exist as public institutions?

Just as multiculturalism raises the fear of divisiveness introduced into what we perhaps unrealistically recall as a more homogeneous society, so too does the rise of conservative and fundamentalist Christian groups. They create their own schools in many communities, and the separate schools of religious groups—such as the widespread system of Catholic schools—have often raised fears that those raised within them would not be as good Americans, would not be as well attuned to the distinctive qualities of American life as those who attended public schools. In the case of the Catholic schools these fears have abated. Not so in the case of the Christian schools. The fear is even greater that the election of fundamentalist Christians to school boards will change the public school, with prayer regularly introduced, the teaching of evolution banned, and a narrow-minded point of view imposed in regard to roles for women or tolerance for gays and lesbians. Around these issues battles rage in scores of school districts in the United States and regularly reach that pinnacle of final decision making, the Supreme Court.

The fear that the new multiculturalism and diversity, as well as the new religious conservatism, will impose terrible strains on the fabric of American life is widespread among American political, cultural, and social elites. And indeed the strains are real and strong. We will be a more "diverse" and in consequence a more divided country. But it is a country in which all parties, I believe, still agree that they should play by the same rules, those hammered out more than two centuries ago and still evolving under the American constitutional system. That is the saving note.

Notes

1. According to a data base that records the texts of leading American newspapers. See Bernstein, *The Dictatorship of Virtue: Multiculturalism and the Battle for America's Future* (New York: Knopf, 1994).

2. See Seymour Martin Lipset, *The First New Nation: The United States in Historical and Comparative Perspective* (New York: Basic Books, 1963).

3. See Philip Gleason, *Speaking of Diversity: Language and Diversity in Twentieth Century America* (Baltimore: Johns Hopkins University Press, 1992), pp. 5–6.

4. "NEA Backing for Gay Month Sparks Firestorm," *Education Week*, 25 October 1995, p. 3.

UNIVERSITY PRESS OF NEW ENGLAND

publishes books under its own imprint and is the publisher for Brandeis University Press, Dartmouth College, Middlebury College Press, University of New Hampshire, Tufts University, Wesleyan University Press, and Salzburg Seminar.

Library of Congress Cataloging-in-Publication Data

Religion, ethnicity, and self-identity : nations in turmoil / Martin
    E. Marty and R. Scott Appleby, editors.
    p.   cm.
    "Salzburg Seminar books."
    ISBN 0–87451–815–6 (cloth : alk. paper)
      1. Nationalism—Religious aspects.   2. Ethnicity—Religious
aspects.   3. Religious fundamentalism.   4. Identification (Religion)
5. Religion and international affairs.   6. World politics—1989–
I. Marty, Martin E., 1928–   .   II. Appleby, R. Scott, 1956–   .
BL65.N3R46   1997
322′.1′09—dc21   96–37268